Living

at the

LAKE

Living at the Lake

Marilyn D. Bachmann

•

Mark V. Hoyer

•

Daniel E. Canfield, Jr.

UNIVERSITY OF
FLORIDA

Institute of Food and Agricultural Sciences

Living at the Lake – A Handbook for Florida Lakefront Property Owners (SP 247)
Marilyn D. Bachmann, Mark V. Hoyer, and Daniel E. Canfield, Jr.

© 1999 University of Florida, Institute of Food and Agricultural Sciences (IFAS) and the Florida Cooperative Extension Service,
    PO Box 110810 Gainesville, Florida 32610-0810

Printed in the United States of America.
ISBN 0-916287-29-7
FIRST EDITION

Editor: Charles Brown
Art Direction: Audrey S. Wynne
Graphic Design: Billie Hermansen
Cover Photo: Thomas Wright

– of related interest

Florida LAKEWATCH by Daniel E. Canfield, Jr. Learn about the citizen-volunteer organization that started in Florida and became a model for the nation. With this book , you can learn about the mission of Lakewatch and how to get involved. IFAS Publication SP-137.

Florida LAKEWATCH Video. Travel some of Florida's lakes with staff and volunteers and see Lakewatch volunteers and professional staff at work. IFAS Video SV-438.

Florida Freshwater Plants: A Handbook of Common Aquatic Plants in Florida Lakes, by M.V. Hoyer, D.E. Canfield, Jr., C. Horsburgh, and K. Brown. This book catalogs 100+ plants found in Florida lakes from Pensacola to Miami. Essential information on each species is provided: color photographs, botanical descriptions, species' biology and ecology, and maps giving the plant's location throughout Florida. This coverage is extended with water chemistries for plant growth and extensive bibliographic references. IFAS Publication SP-189.

Resources Catalog. Books, manuals, videos, CD-ROMs, flash cards, and other media related to natural science and food resources are available from the University of Florida's Institute of Food and Agricultural Sciences. IFAS Publication SP-1.
Visit our website at: http://ems.ifas.ufl.edu/ForSale
Any resource may be ordered by contacting:
IFAS Publications Distribution Center
University of Florida
PO Box 110011
Gainesville, Florida 32611-0011
(800) 226-1764

What is Extension?

The Cooperative Extension Service is a partnership of county, state, and federal government which serves the citizens of Florida by providing information and training on a wide variety of topics. In Florida, the Extension Service is a part of the University of Florida's Institute of Food and Agricultural Sciences with selected programs at Florida Agricultural and Mechanical University (FAMU). Extension touches almost everyone in the state from the homeowner to huge agribusiness operations in such areas as: food safety, gardening, child and family development, consumer credit counseling, youth development, energy conservation, sustainable agriculture, competitiveness in world markets, and natural resource conservation.

COOPERATIVE EXTENSION SERVICE, UNIVERSITY OF FLORIDA, INSTITUTE OF FOOD AND AGRICULTURAL SCIENCES, Christine Taylor Waddill, Dean, in cooperation with the United States Department of Agriculture, publishes this information to further the purpose of the May 8 and June 30, 1914 Acts of Congress; and is authorized to provide research, educational information and other services only to individuals and institutions that function without regard to race, color, age, sex, handicap or national origin. The information in this publication is available in alternate formats. Information on copies for purchase is available from IFAS Publications Distribution Center, University of Florida, PO Box 110011, Gainesville, Florida 32611-0011. Information about alternate formats is available from IFAS Educational Media and Services, University of Florida, PO Box 110810, Gainesville, Florida 32611-0810. This information was published Nov. 1998 as SP-247, Florida Cooperative Extension Service.

Table of Contents

Acknowledgments

The authors wish to acknowledge the influence that the book *Life on the Edge* (1994) by M. Dresen and R. Korth and published by the University of Wisconsin had on the writing of this book. This excellent handbook for Wisconsin lakefront property owners was both the stimulus for writing our book and the source of many ideas, including the Checklist for Waterfront Property Buyers, which we have adapted for Florida. We especially thank Ms. Sandy Fisher, Director of Florida LAKEWATCH, for providing a great many of the source materials as well as helpful ideas during the writing of this book. We are grateful for the section on the role of local government included in Chapter 9 which was contributed by Rick Baird, Mike Britt, Kevin McCann, Gene Medley, and Curtis Watkins. We greatly appreciate other materials provided by the Center for Aquatic Plants, University of Florida; the Florida Lake Management Society; UF/IFAS Cooperative Extension Office; the Northwest Florida Water Management District, the St. Johns River Water Management District, the South Florida Water Management District, the Southwest Florida Water Management District, the Suwannee River Water Management District, the Florida Department of Environmental Protection, the U.S. Army Corps of Engineers, and the Florida Game and Fresh Water Fish Commission.

Photography

Marilyn Bachmann
Roger Bachmann
Joan Berish
Mark Brenner
Claude Brown
Mary Cichra
Doug Colle
Mark Hoyer
Frank Kutka
Jeanette Lamb

Robert Lamb
Ken Langeland
Vic Ramey
Amy Richard
Joe Richard
Sal Salazar
Randy Meyers
Thomas Wright
Audrey S. Wynne

Florida Department of Environmental Protection
Florida Game and Fresh Water Fish Commission

CHAPTER 1

Why Live at the Lake

Our many lakes are part of the Florida lifestyle. Owning land on the shores of these lakes brings both the benefits of waterfront living and the responsibilities of lake stewardship.

What draws people to live on the shores of lakes? In a word — Water.

In the past, people were drawn to Florida's lakes because they needed water for survival. Lakes provided water for drinking, household needs, agriculture, industry, and transportation. Lakes also provided food and a cool refuge from Florida's heat — a place to spend summer days.

Today, people decide to live along the lakeshore for various reasons. Some still use the lake to earn a living, but many want the swimming, fishing, boating or jetskiing; others watch wildlife or perhaps get away from urban congestion. Regardless of the reasons, most enjoy simply looking at the water. The view changes constantly throughout the day and with each season; both the sunlight on tranquil, sparkling waters and the rain on wind-driven waves make life interesting at the lake!

Whether you already own lakefront property or are considering a purchase, it is important to ask, "Why do I want to live at the lake?" Do you

dream of swimming in a crystal-clear lake and sunning on a sandy beach? Or do you picture luring a trophy Florida bass out of its hiding place? Perhaps you look forward to recreational boating or waterskiing. Maybe sitting quietly on your dock or in a canoe watching herons fishing or the anhinga drying its wings is part of your vision.

Because all lakes are not the same, not all of them will meet your vision. Some lakes are clear, others murky green or brown. They vary in size and shape, depth, aquatic plant cover, as well as amount and types of development. All these factors affect the ideal uses of a lake and how it will suit your vision.

On one hand, a beautifully clear lake which would be wonderful for swimming may not support fish populations that would provide you with good fishing. On the other hand, a productive lake, perhaps supporting large beds of aquatic plants which provide good fish habitat, may not be best for swimming or recreational boating, but provide good fishing.

Selecting the right lake for your vision is important, but your vision of lake living may change with your experiences and time. You may find life at the lake enjoyable in ways you didn't expect. Children or grandchildren can introduce you to new delights. Changing interests may affect how you live at the lake.

Whatever your vision, life at the lake is not always idyllic; it can be expensive. The higher value of lakefront property means you will pay more for your property initially and continue to pay more every year through higher taxes. How much is it worth to *you* to live on the lakefront?

If you own or are thinking of buying lakefront property, your reasons for doing so may be very important to how you live at the lake or in directing your search for property and making the right choice.

"I like living in a place where there are still dragons."

— R. Hutchinson, Alachua County Conservationist

UF/IFAS Photo Archives

Newnan's Lake is a dark-water lake southeast of Gainesville; it is also a lake of alligators, eagles, and good fishing. The lake is ringed by cypresses, and it is marshy in some areas; lakefront homes occupy only a small percentage of the shoreline. It is considered a great lake for fishing, birding, and observing wildlife. Described as a "wonder," this still-wild lake hasn't changed a great deal since 1812 when Daniel Newnan led his group of volunteers into Alachua County, then a part of Spanish Florida, to destroy Seminole Indian towns. These 250 men were part of an effort by Americans living in Florida to take Florida away from Spain. Their mission was also to punish Indians for harboring runaway slaves and for their burning of plantations on both sides of the St. Johns River. Camped very close to the lake named after him, Newnan and his volunteers endured seven days "surviving on horseflesh, alligators, and palm hearts." After several skirmishes during which Newnan was ill with fever, the volunteers were rescued. Although the group did not succeed in either of its missions, its members were cited for their bravery for the suffering they had endured. Daniel Newnan served as a member of the U.S. Congress from Georgia from 1831-33. Newnan's Lake, while still relatively undeveloped and natural, has water quality and algal problems which are being studied. Concern for the lake has several agencies considering plans for protecting the lake. Meanwhile, the "dragons" continue to float on the lake surface — the prehistoric-looking gators provide a link with the past, reminding us of the long history of the region and of people who once lived along and fished this lake.

(Sources: "A creepy place where dragons linger and eagles soar;" Ron Cunningham; Gainesville Sun; Sunday, November 16,1997; page 3G and "Newnan: Soldier, Statesman;" John K. Mahon; Gainesville Sun; Sunday, November 16, 1997; page 3G.)

People enjoy lakes in many different ways, and their activities are not always compatible. If your hobbies include power boating or jetskiing, but your neighbors like to fish, watch wildlife or canoe in quiet waters, conflict is probable.

Life on the lakefront means stewardship as well as enjoyment. Our Florida lakes are enjoyed by citizens whether they live nearby or visit on the weekends. Lakefront owners have a special responsibility, not only to their neighbors, but to wildlife and the natural environment.

Living at the lake is an adventure. You will interact with changing environmental conditions, interesting wildlife, a variety of people and many governmental agencies. You may need to become familiar with lake ecology, managing your lakefront property, and the laws and regulations that affect you and your lake. You also will need to understand how lakes can be managed and protected. Learning more about your lake will increase your enjoyment and appreciation.

We hope the information assembled in this book will help you, a present or prospective lakefront property owner in Florida.

Did you know...

The dragonflies which you see flitting around the plants on your lakeshore actually spend part of their lives (up to a year) living on the lake bottom and among the plants before they emerge as adults.

For More Information…

Florida Lake Management Society's Lakes Information Resource Guide.
   1996. Florida Lake Management Society. Lakeland, Fla.
Florida Lakes: A Description of Lakes, Their Processes and Means of Protection.
   by H. Lee Edmiston and V.B. Myers. Water Quality Management and Restoration,
   Department of Environmental Regulation, Tallahassee, Fla. Wilderness Graphics,
   Inc. Tallahassee, Fla. 1983.
NALMS Management Guide for Lakes and Reservoirs.
   North American Lake Management Society. Madison, Wis.
What Makes a Quality Lake?
   by D.E. Canfield, Jr. Institute of Food and Agricultural Sciences, University of Florida.
   Gainesville, Fla. Florida Cooperative Extension Service videotape SV-398. 24 min. ❧

Mark V. Hoyer

Who can resist the smile of a child with a fish?

CHAPTER 2

What Makes a Good Lake

*...All lakes are not created equal, but all are good lakes
for someone or some purpose.*

Once you have decided that you would like to live on a lake, what kind of lake do you want? A "good lake," of course, you answer. Everyone looking for waterfront property wants to live on a "good lake," but what makes a lake "good" to one person may make it less useful or attractive to someone else. It depends on what expectations you have for lake living.

Let's suppose, for example, you want a view of clear, sparkling water. Most people find clear water very beautiful, but it may be a disadvantage if you are interested in abundant fish and wildlife. That lovely clear water may well be nutrient poor and unable to support large fish or wildlife populations. On the other hand, nutrient-rich lakes can support abundant fish and wildlife, increasing the quality of the lake for fishing and bird watching. But these lakes can produce heavy algal or aquatic plant (macrophyte) growth — all those weeds! — that cause problems for boaters and swimmers. So, before you rank a lake as bad or good, you must first decide how you want to use the lake and what you expect to gain from living along its shores.

Lakes vary naturally in origin, size, water chemistry, plant and animal populations, and a host of other characteristics. Depending on how you wish to use the lake, each of these characteristics could increase or decrease the value of a lakefront property to you. You might not understand what all these characteristics are, so in this chapter we explain some important lake characteristics and some lake ecology. This will help you understand differences between lakes and determine which kind of lake would be best for you.

Lake Origins

Florida has over 7000 lakes, some very small and some, such as Lake Okeechobee, very large. Maybe you've never thought about how these lakes got here, but there are different ways that lakes get started. Most Florida lakes are "solution lakes." The formation of these lakes begins when limestone under the surface dissolves and creates an underground cave or cavity. When the land over the cavity collapses, the resulting cavity can fill with water, and a lake is born. We often see the beginning of this process when sinkholes form; usually a lake which starts like this will be quite round, but if a sinkhole develops in a valley, erosion forms an elongated basin. Other lakes are simply depressions in an irregular topography or former seabeds filled with freshwater, like Lake Okeechobee. Lakes can form when looping river meanders are cut off from the main channel (oxbows). Lakes can form from wide areas of river channels, for example, Lake George, and from floodplains of rivers. We also have man-made lakes, such as Lake Seminole in Gadsden County, Lake Rousseau, and

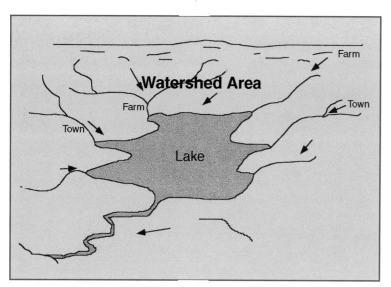

Rodman Reservoir; some of these lakes are produced by damming rivers, and others from excavations, borrow pits or mining.

Lake Trophic Status

It has been said that all lakes are individuals, but they do have similarities which allow us to group them loosely into categories and make some generalizations. One of the most important factors used to group lakes is the total level of plant production (both vascular plants and algae). The technical term used for this plant production in lakes is "lake trophic status." The trophic status system allows scientists to group lakes into four types or trophic states:

- oligotrophic — low plant production
- mesotrophic — moderate plant production
- eutrophic — high plant production
- hypereutrophic — extremely high plant production

Macrophytes on Lake Lochloosa

In order to grow, plants use energy from the sun through a process called photosynthesis. Green aquatic plants (primary producers) gather the sun's energy, trapping it as chemical fuel which in turn becomes the basic energy source for everything else that lives in the lake. Therefore, the total amount of animal life including invertebrates, amphibians, reptiles, fish and other wildlife in a lake depends on the total amount of plant production. Oligotrophic lakes with their low plant production also have low animal production. Hypereutrophic lakes are on the other end of the trophic state scale; they have high plant production and correspondingly high animal production.

Why are some lakes low producers while others are high producers? Simply put, high producing lakes have more of the things plants need to grow. Plants surely need to get enough sunlight to grow, but photosynthesizing aquatic plants (both macrophytes and algae) need nutrients as well as sunlight to grow and reproduce. Two of the important nutrients needed by plants, phosphorus and nitrogen, are found both in lake sediments and dissolved in the water. These are generally in short supply in oligotrophic (low producing) lakes; such lakes cannot support large populations of plants, and therefore cannot support large animal populations either. On the other end of the trophic state scale, hypereutrophic (very high producing) lakes generally have abundant phosphorus and nitrogen to support extensive aquatic plant growth which, in turn, can support animals.

Phosphorus, rather than nitrogen, has been shown most often to be the limiting nutrient in lakes that holds back abundant growth of plants. When more phosphorus becomes available, either the aquatic plants (macrophytes) or the plankton algae will increase.

Though phosphorus is often the limiting nutrient, if something else that plants need for growth, for example, light, is in even shorter supply than phosphorus, we refer to that substance or condition as "limiting". Thus, in our example, increases in phosphorus under low light conditions would not increase aquatic plant growth.

So, one environmental factor may act to limit another. For another example, in areas where springs continuously gush large volumes of water, the water moves too fast for planktonic algae to accumulate to the level that would be expected from the amount of nutrients present. Even though phosphorus and nitrogen are abundant, plant growth is low. Similarly, if a lake has a fast flushing rate (the fraction of the lake volume leaving through its outlet each year), the water may move out faster than the algae or macrophytes can use the nutrients. Another example occurs in lakes with high levels of suspended particles (turbidity). These particles can shade the lower

This lakefront has extensive beds of aquatic plants.

levels of the lake, preventing algae or macrophytes from growing even when phosphorus is abundant. In this case, light is the limiting factor.

Eutrophication

The process by which lakes can change from one trophic state to a higher one through nutrient enrichment is called eutrophication. This is a natural process brought about by the filling in of the lake basin by sediments from the lake's watershed, and the accumulation of nutrients. This is a slow process which ordinarily takes thousands, if not tens of thousands, of years. Human activities which increase inputs of nutrients and/or particulates from eroding soils or treated effluent from sewage plants also can cause eutrophication to proceed faster than would occur naturally (this is called cultural eutrophication). Lakes which are undergoing eutrophication will show accompanying changes in the amounts and diversity of animal and plant life.

Both natural and human-caused changes are important to lakefront property owners and prospective buyers. You need to realize that without some type of lake management your lake may not stay the same.

Lake Regions

It has been said that lakes are only as good as the water coming into them. Where does the water entering a lake come from? In most lakes, the majority of the water entering a lake comes from runoff from the lake's watershed (the surrounding land area that drains into the lake). If the watershed of the lake has soils that are easily eroded, water entering the lake will be full of sediment and, most likely, nutrients associated with the sediments.

Regional differences in soil types are responsible for many of the differences in trophic state among Florida lakes. The soils where lakes and their

Where does the water entering a lake come from?

• • •

In most lakes, the majority of the water entering a lake comes from runoff from the lake's watershed.

watersheds are located may be very different as you compare lakes throughout the state. In Florida, many lakes lie among depressions in sand ridges (examples: Ocala National Forest, Lake Wales Ridge, and Washington County) and are filled by water that seeps over and through the sand. These lakes are generally very clear, with low levels of nutrients resulting in low levels of primary plant production and animal life. Many other lakes have high levels of plant nutrients because their waters originate in nutrient-rich soils, swamps, or natural deposits of phosphate rocks (for example, the phosphate mining area around Lakeland, Florida). These lakes are higher in productivity, with more algae and/or aquatic plants and animal life. The important thing to remember is that the type of watershed in which your lake exists will have a strong impact on whether your lake is naturally clear and nutrient poor or naturally green and nutrient rich.

The United States Environmental Protection Agency (U.S. EPA) has gone beyond differentiating lake types by watershed differences and recently divided the State of Florida into 47 lake regions. Each region was determined by similarity of factors such as physiology, geology, hydrology, and water chemistry values. A copy of the publication entitled *Lake Regions of Florida* can be obtained from EPA (contact EPA for publication no. EPA.R-97-127). This publication should be extremely helpful if you want to live on a specific type of lake.

Water Clarity and General Water Chemistry

Water samples, along with measurements within the lake itself, can provide a variety of useful information about your lake. There are many analyses and procedures used to provide this information, as you will find if you decide to learn more than we can summarize here. There are veritable libraries of text books and manuals on the subject. Let's discuss a few of these variables that you will

A Secchi disk disappears quickly in a lake with an algal bloom.

probably be confronted with if you live on or are planning to live on a lake.

Water Clarity. Water clarity is the first thing most people notice when they walk up to a lake, and the one that imparts a lasting memory of a lake. Water clarity is usually measured with a Secchi disk, a black and white disk about eight inches in diameter. The Secchi disk is lowered into the water until you can no longer see it; that depth is called the Secchi depth and is used as a measure of water clarity.

If a lake were filled with distilled water, the Secchi disk would still be visible at 120 feet down. Real lake water, however, is not that transparent; dissolved and suspended materials reduce light transmission so you can't see nearly that far down. Some lakes have a brown stain due to dissolved organic substances, other lakes have suspended particles either washed in from the watershed or resuspended from the lake bottom by wind-driven waves, and all have some suspended algae. All of these materials reduce water transparency and decrease the depth at which you can see into the lake, thus reducing the Secchi depth measurement of "water clarity."

For many lakes, water clarity is determined primarily by the abundance of suspended algae. So water clarity will be low in hypereutrophic lakes with abundant algae; the Secchi depth will usually be less than three feet. Conversely, water clarity will be high in oligotrophic lakes with low algal populations; you will usually be able to see the Secchi disk at depths greater than 13 feet.

Did you know…

…why you can't see Lake Okeechobee as you approach it? Lake Okeechobee is unusual among our lakes in having a dike around it. The lake was diked after the hurricanes of 1926 and 1928. Hurricane winds pushed the water out of the lake, flooding towns and killing over 2400 people in the area. Wildlife also were killed, including hundreds of alligators, and many of Lake Okeechobee's fish were left stranded when the waters receded.

A Simple Solution: The Secchi Disk

How do you measure the transparency (or clarity) of your lake? You may have watched biologists or citizen volunteers lower a small disk painted in black and white quadrants into the lake (the disk may also be all white). Water clarity can be determined by measuring the distance from the water's surface to the depth at which the disk is no longer visible. In this age of technology and complex (as well as expensive) scientific apparatus, this simple disk is providing water quality information as it has for nearly 140 years. This elegant and simple device was developed in 1865 when the commander of Pope Pius IX's steam corvette engaged Professor P.A. Secchi. The commander employed Secchi to study the use of a white disk for measuring water in the Mediterranean Sea. Secchi's study was published in the commander's report, and it established the experimental procedure for obtaining transparency with a Secchi disk, as it is called today.

Eagle Eye, Inc

Oligotrophic lakes are not the only ones where you see clear water. If you take your canoe or boat out onto a shallow, highly productive lake that is filled with beds of large plants, you can also look down into clear water. Lakes with an abundance of large aquatic plants often have clear water and few algae suspended in the water. One reason for this is that most algae require water movements to keep them from settling to the bottom. The large plants (macrophytes) reduce the ability of the wind to stir the water and keep the algae suspended.

Macrophytes also decrease the suspended algae populations by preventing wind or wave action from resuspending bottom sediments. Another factor is that large aquatic plants, together with their attached algae, compete with the suspended algae for nutrients and light. The plants may also harbor microscopic swimming animals called zooplankton which feed on algae.

Thus, aquatic plants can maintain clear water in several ways, and even a hypereutrophic lake will have clear water if the plant production of the lake is dominated by large plants instead of suspended algae. If the macrophytes are removed from such a lake, the water may become less clear due to resuspension of bottom sediments and growth of suspended algae. Such changes have occurred when plants were lost due to high water levels, storms, or intentional total plant removal with grass carp, mechanical removal, or herbicides. This can happen rather quickly (perhaps in only a few months) with the result that the lake switches from a lake covered by large aquatic plants to a green and/or turbid lake with an abundance of suspended algae.

This relationship between large aquatic plants and water clarity is an important one to understand for anyone living or planning to live on a lake. Many Florida lakes are "blessed" with abundant large aquatic plants (see

Lakes with an abundance of large aquatic plants often have clear water and few algae suspended in the water.

Chapter 4), and aquatic plant control is one of the major management activities occurring on these lakes. With the control of aquatic plants there is the potential for large changes in water clarity. Therefore, if you are hoping to live on a lake with clear water, and you find one with abundant large aquatic plants, the lake has the potential to lose its clear water if enough aquatic plants are removed or naturally disappear.

Lake Color. The actual color of lake water is determined by the type of suspended particles and substances that are dissolved in the water. Suspended algae can add several different colors to the water because of the kinds of pigments that they possess, but most algae will give your lake a green color. Decaying vegetation and other organic matter suspended in the water can give varying colors of black and brown to lake water depending on the stage of decomposition and water chemistry of the lake. Suspended clay particles can make the water gray to reddish depending on the geology of the area in which the lake exists.

The water in some lakes may be stained a light yellow to dark brown, tea color. This is caused by organic humic materials that originate from soils in the drainage basin. For example, water coming to a lake from cypress swamps is often deeply stained with these materials. This is natural and is not an indication of pollution. Stained lake water may not be as attractive for swimming, but it does not detract from other uses.

You may see foam on the surface of the water, especially in dark-water lakes after heavy rain. Organic materials, such as tannin, which have washed into the water can break down into substances that are like the fatty acids in soap. Wind and waves may cause the foam to form streaks on the surface (called Langmuir streaks). This is natural and not a sign that the lake is deteriorating.

The actual color of lake water is determined by the type of suspended particles and substances that are dissolved in the water.

In the spring, you also might see a yellow powder floating on your lake, sometimes so much that the lake appears to be yellow (often looking like yellow paint). This is primarily pine pollen which, while it may accumulate on shorelines along with other floating debris, will decompose and go away. Other things, such as masses of the alga *Lyngbya*, can cause areas of the lake to appear yellow, orange, or red.

Chlorophyll Concentration. We have already discussed the nutrients phosphorus and nitrogen (which are also considered water chemistry variables) and their direct relationship to algal population abundance. Algal abundance is also related to water clarity. It is difficult and time consuming, however, to actually count algal cells in lake water. Instead, most lake sampling programs measure concentrations of algal chlorophyll in a measured volume of water. Chlorophylls are pigments common to all green plants and measuring the amount of chlorophyll in lake water yields an estimate of algal abundance.

A technician prepares water samples for analysis.

Lake Trophic Status	Total Nitrogen (μg/L)	Phosphorus (μg/L)	Total Chlorophyll a (μg/L)	Secchi Depth (meters)
Oligotrophic	<400	<15	<3	>4.0
Mesotrophic	400-600	15-25	3-7	2.5-4.0
Eutrophic	600-1500	25-100	7-40	1.0-2.5
Hypereutrophic	>1500	>100	>40	<1.0

Lake Trophic State Variables. Total phosphorus, total nitrogen, chlorophyll concentrations, and water clarity are the four primary variables used to classify a lake's trophic status. A classic example of this is the above lake classification system used by C. Forsberg and S. Ryding in 1980. This and other classification systems work well for most lakes until a lake has abundant large aquatic plants or some factor other than phosphorus or nitrogen limits the growth of aquatic plants and algae.

Acidity and Alkalinity. Another important variable of lake water which can be measured is pH, which indicates whether the water is acidic or basic. When we measure the pH of the water sample from our lake, we are measuring hydrogen ions dissolved in the water. The more hydrogen ions, the more acidic the water is and the lower the pH: a pH of 7 is neutral; higher pH measurements mean the water is alkaline (or basic).

Most Florida lakes have a pH between 4 and 9. Aquatic animals do well in waters which are somewhat acidic to slightly basic — from about 6.5 to 9. However, some species are more tolerant than others; one species may do better in an acid lake and another less well, leading to differences, for example, in the dominant fish populations.

Changes in acidity also can cause release of toxic materials through chemical reactions of substances in the water. Aluminum released from bottom sediments can be taken up by aquatic animals, increase acidity resulting in higher carbon dioxide levels, and raise the corrosiveness of the water. One common means of raising pH is by liming, which adds alkaline components to offset the acidity.

Alkalinity measures the presence of substances such as carbonates and bicarbonates in the water. These substances act as buffers (which can

Marilyn D. Bachmann

Researchers collect algae in a marsh.

neutralize acids) to protect animals from sudden pH changes. Measurements are in equivalents of calcium carbonate; average alkalinity measurements in Florida lakes range from 0 to about 200 mg/L.

Hardness. Many people have well water or municipal water which is "hard", leaving scaly deposits on faucets and shower walls. Lakes, too, can be "hard" or "soft" depending upon the amount of materials such as calcium and magnesium their water contains. When limestone (calcium carbonate) comes in contact with slightly acidic water, the rock is dissolved, releasing the calcium; therefore, lakes in limestone areas are likely to be "hard".

Hardness measurements are in terms of equivalents of calcium carbonate. Florida lakes range from an average of 2–720 mg/L. Most of our lakes (75%) are "softwater" lakes, with a total hardness measurement of less than 40 mg/L.

Dissolved Oxygen. Oxygen gas dissolved in water allows aquatic animals to survive in the lake and is particularly critical for fish survival. Aquatic plants, through photosynthesis, produce (and also, through respiration, use) oxygen. The amount of oxygen in the water varies on a daily basis, rising on a sunny day as plants photosynthesize and dropping at night. It also varies with the amount of wind, which moves and mixes the water, adding oxygen. We measure oxygen levels as mg/L (or ppm). As levels of dissolved oxygen go below 3–4 mg/L, the ability of aquatic animals to survive goes down.

Did you know...

In the first half of this century, Lake Apopka was one of the premier bass fishing lakes in the United States. At that time, the lake had extensive beds of aquatic plants which served as good fish habitat. Many fishing camps operated along the lake's shore; fishermen followed regular paths through the plant beds to reach their favorite spots.

If the lake has large masses of aquatic plants, their positive ability to produce oxygen is offset by the oxygen lost as bacteria decompose large amounts of organic debris formed by dying plants. When large areas of plants die off at the same time, for example, at the end of a particular season, fish kills can result as decomposition causes the oxygen levels to drop. The dead plants may also shade other plants below them, causing them to die and dissolved oxygen levels to drop lower.

In a lake which has a great deal of organic matter, bacterial breakdown of this material will use much of the dissolved oxygen, reducing the amount available to aquatic animals. By measuring the organic material in the water, we can determine the amount of oxygen which will be used in breakdown (called BOD or Biochemical Oxygen Demand).

Levels of dissolved oxygen also fluctuate with water temperature, since warm water holds less than cool water. This is an important factor in determining which fish species survive in lakes in hot seasons or climates. Some species such as bowfin and gar can live in warm waters which have very low levels of dissolved oxygen. They are adapted to surface breathing if conditions get bad. Mosquitofish, which have mouths adapted to get oxygen from the air-water interface, also do well. Other species, such as shad, are much less tolerant and more likely to die if dissolved oxygen levels get too low.

Before You Buy...

When considering property on a particular lake, take a boat ride and get a good look at the lake. You may be able to see 10 or more feet down in a clear lake, less in more productive ones. Sandy bottoms and beaches are more common in oligotrophic lakes. Look at the shoreline to see how much aquatic plant growth there is and whether there are areas of excessive algal growth.

When considering property on a particular lake, take a boat ride and get a good look at the lake.

Look for indications of past high or low water marks. You might be able to see indications of old shorelines or tell something by the positioning or species of trees near the shore. For example, cypress trees suggest past higher water levels since young trees need water to get established). Ask the neighbors what the lake was like last year (or in the past if they have lived there a long time) or at other seasons of the year.

Which type of lake is right for you? Think about your expected recreational activities relative to the lake being considered. Consider the importance of swimming beaches, boating, fishing, and opportunities to observe wildlife. Perhaps the clear lake with sandy beaches isn't necessary or best for you.

For More Information...

Florida Lakes: A Description of Lakes, Their Processes and Means of Protection.
   by H. Lee Edmiston and V.B. Myers. 1983. Water Quality Management and Restoration, Dept. of Environmental Regulation, Tallahassee, Fla. Wilderness Graphics, Inc. Tallahassee, Fla.
What Makes a Quality Lake?
   by D.E. Canfield, Jr. Institute of Food and Agricultural Sciences, University of Florida. Gainesville, Fla. Florida Cooperative Extension Service videotape SV-398. 24 min.
NALMS Management Guide for Lakes and Rivers.
   North American Lake Management Society. Madison, Wis.
Volunteer Lake Monitoring: A Methods Manual.
   by J.T. Simpson. 1991. U.S. Environmental Protection Agency. Washington, DC. EPA publication 440/4-91-002.
Restoration and Management of Lakes and Reservoirs, 2d edition.
   by G. Dennis Cooke. 1993. Lewis Publishers. New York. 548 pp. ❧

Mark Brenner

Residents enjoy recreational boating on Lake Conway.

CHAPTER 3

Your Wildlife Neighbors

...Enjoy the woods and life at the lake,
but keep your eyes peeled for gator and snake!

We like to live on lakes, and many of us are thrilled to be so close to the diverse wildlife in our state. By building a home in the woods near the water, Florida's many wild animals and birds become our next-door neighbors. Like any neighbors, their behaviors and habits may come into conflict with our activities. We want to enjoy the many fascinating animals and plants. (Suggestions to attract wildlife such as hummingbirds and butterflies have been presented in Chapter 7.) We also may need to control the activities and populations of some. We offer you a few of our ideas related to getting along with wildlife.

Be Alert!... See it First!

It is always a good idea to be alert when you are working, playing, or just out for a stroll in the woods or near water. It is particularly true here in Florida, where the great diversity of animal and plant species include some which are annoying and some which are dangerous. If you grew up in Florida, you know not to stand in a fire ant nest and to keep an eye out for snakes.

Living at the lake, particularly if you are in more rural settings, brings you into close association with many of these plants and animals. Keeping your eyes open for what is around you and on the ground where you are stepping can help you avoid problems.

Scales and No Scales

Please Don't Feed the Alligators! Sooner or later, almost everyone living on a lake sees a "gator". They are perhaps as symbolic of Florida as oranges or beaches. Alligators now number over a million in the state, a long way from their population lows several decades ago. With their prehistoric look and their link with the dinosaurs of long ago, they fascinate many and strike fear into others.

What will you do when you find gators in your front yard or down by the dock? Hopefully, you will neither panic nor decide to make a pet of one. Fortunately, they are generally not aggressive, preferring to bask in the sunshine; however, they can move very fast and their jaws are very powerful. It is unwise, therefore, to approach one too closely or to put your child near it to take a picture!

Never feed that gator! If you do, you will have "signed its death warrant", for it will come back for food, approaching you for its handout, and may injure you or others in the process. Gators may not be particularly intelligent, but they do remember where a handout was given. If you feed a gator, it is almost certain that it will become a "nuisance alligator" and will have to be destroyed.

Learn to be alert, so that you don't approach an alligator unexpectedly. They are a very interesting part of our wildlife, but observe them from a distance. For your safety, don't swim in areas near gators or where you don't know what might be living there. Be especially careful during the spring

Marilyn D. Bachmann

A gator basks in the sun at the water's edge.

Gators: Florida's Dragons

Was an alligator the original model for the mythical Chinese dragons? Some scholars think so. In Florida, a gator might be seen any place where there is water. (Gators are also University of Florida sports team members and their fans!) The alligator's prehistoric look both scares and fascinates people.

Alligators are just one species of the Crocodilians, the only living representatives of the group to which the dinosaurs belonged, but their prehistoric look is misleading. In many ways, including temperature regulation and care of their young, the gator is anything but primitive. Lacking the ability to produce enough heat to maintain body temperature on their own (as people and other mammals can), gators use special behaviors to keep themselves from becoming too warm or too cool. Basking in the sun on the bank or floating on the surface, the gator is absorbing heat. That open mouth you see is probably not a sign of aggression but a behavior that brings the gator's body temperature down through evaporative cooling.

Fortunately, alligators (unlike some other species of crocodiles) are not normally aggressive. However, you should be wary of male alligators in the breeding season and females guarding their nests. In the spring, when temperatures and day length are just right, hormones build up in male alligators, and bellowing and aggressive behaviors rise. Female hormones also increase, and mating follows. Eggs are laid in the prepared nests in early June in Florida, and the female remains with the eggs. Parental care in alligators is well developed; the female guards the nest throughout incubation, protecting eggs and new young from predation. If you approach too close to her nest, she may consider you a predator and react accordingly!

From inside the mounded nest come sounds which tell the female alligator her young are about to hatch. Inside the nest, the young gators push their snouts against the eggshells to break them and emerge. The female breaks open the nest, then takes each unhatched egg in her mouth, cracking the shell to assist hatching. She may then carry her newly hatched young to water and stay with them for many months. Remember that although baby gators are cute, they do bite. If you happen to snag a baby gator while fishing or hear little alarm sounds, look around for Mama Gator and make yourself scarce! Mama Gator may come to the rescue.

mating season when bull alligators are likely to be aggressive. If you let your pets wander along vegetated edges of lakes and rivers, gators might see them as food. If you have a problem gator, call your local wildlife officer.

Snake-in-the-grass. Florida wildlife includes many species of snakes, including some which are poisonous. Many kinds of snakes are valuable for their appetite for rats and mice, and most are harmless. Learn to recognize those which are dangerous and avoid situations which might lead to snakebite.

Some of our snakes are poisonous. Several species of rattlesnakes, the cottonmouth or water moccasin, the copperhead (parts of the Panhandle only), and the coral snake are found in the state. Watching where you walk, not stepping over logs or putting your hands in vegetation where you can't see what is there, and listening for warning rattles will help you avoid these snakes. Piles of brush may attract snakes by providing cover.

These snakes are almost hidden in the grass along the shore.

Leave gopher tortoise burrows alone; rattlesnakes may share these burrows. The coral snake is secretive and may live for years in an area and never be seen. Its bright yellow, red, and black coloration make it easy to spot. (The similarly colored scarlet king snake does not have a black snout and has a different color order in its banding.) Never handle it, and teach your children not to approach or touch these animals.

The cottonmouth is most likely encountered near the water's edge, especially if there is thick vegetation. Eastern Diamondback rattlesnakes also can be encountered near water as they forage for food. Listening for the warning rattle and being alert will help you avoid contact with these snakes.

Turtles and Tortoises. Nearly everyone loves turtles, those "tanks on legs", and there are many kinds of turtles here in Florida. You will see aquatic turtles basking along riverbanks, sometimes more than a hundred in a group. You may also see them in your front yard, moving up from the lake to lay their eggs. Watch for them when mowing and try to avoid disturbing the female while she is laying her eggs. It is fascinating to watch the egg-laying process, and if you mark the spot, you will be rewarded to see the tiny hatchlings as they emerge from the nest later in the summer and head for the water.

If part of your property away from the lake is high and dry, you may also find the burrows of gopher tortoises (a land turtle) and watch them as they go around in their daily foraging. Their burrows are usually obvious because of the sandy approach. Tortoises rarely bite and, if not disturbed, soon become less wary and accustomed to you. Many homeowners in Florida have a resident tortoise or two on their property. They are protected by law — observe but don't disturb!

Voices in the Night. Ever hear the story of the couple who came to Florida and were very upset about the loud noises coming from their backyard? The noises were so loud they couldn't sleep. The biologist from the university told them those were frogs! The numbers of frogs in Florida, many of them tree frogs, are in the "zillions".

Turtles warm up in the warm Florida sunshine.

Unlike the couple in the story, who returned to their former home because they couldn't stand the noise, most people enjoy frogs. You'll increase your appreciation if you become acquainted with different kinds of frogs and learn to recognize each species by its call. A recording of the calls of Florida frogs is available from the Florida Museum of Natural History at the University of Florida.

Many of the frogs are difficult to see; one, the Little Grass Frog, is the smallest frog in North America, measuring about 2/3 of an inch. It is a real challenge to see one, even when it is calling right next to you. Especially on wet spring nights, you will see tree frogs on the sides of buildings, on the outsides of doors and windows (and sometimes inside). Feeding on small insects, they are useful as well as fascinating animals.

With Fur or Feathers

Dam Builders. In northern parts of Florida, people living on or near streams can have "beaver problems." The beaver's tendency to build dams across waterways, creating flooded areas, can cause problems for you. They may also cut down trees near the water. In the right places, their activities can be interesting to observe, and the ponds they create are useful for fish and other wildlife. In other situations, they become a nuisance. Your local wildlife officer can advise you, either in solving beaver problems or attracting them.

"Sandy-mounders." This is another name for the Pocket Gopher, a rodent about 10 inches long, which can cause garden, crop, or landscape damage by its activities. If you have numerous large sandy mounds on your property, the "sandy-mounder" may be the culprit.

One pocket gopher can be responsible for as many as 50 of these mounds which, when they occur in natural areas, are beneficial to the sandhill ecosystem and the many animals which live in the tunnels. If they are damaging your property, you can legally trap them without a permit. It is, however, illegal to poison them without a Poison Permit from the Game and Fresh Water Fish Commission. See below for more information on trapping and exclusion techniques.

Nutria. Introduced from South America for the fur trade, nutria are large aquatic mammals (beaver-like rodents which weigh 8–18 pounds). They have spread into many states, including Florida. Here they found few natural

A frog sits placidly on a lilypad waiting for a meal.

Marilyn D. Bachmann

predators and good habitat, they thrived and spread in the diverse aquatic habitats, including canals and polluted waters. They have now spread throughout much of Florida. While they do eat undesirable aquatic plants, they can completely denude a pond or small lake to the point where even they can't live there. The State of Florida passed a law in 1959 (Florida Statute 372.98) prohibiting the release of nutria (*Myocastor coypu*), restricting possession of these animals for any reason without a permit, and setting requirements for nutria farmers regarding licenses and housing. Nutria can denude aquatic vegetation; their burrowing can damage canals and highway culverts and break levees, flooding croplands in some areas.

Duck! Ducks and geese are fun to watch, especially when they have families of little fuzzy ducklings and goslings swimming behind them. It is tempting to feed them to attract them and enjoy watching their behavior. However, there are disadvantages to this. Both ducks and geese are messy, and the droppings they leave on your lawn (or your neighbors) are squishy if you step in them and can be smelly if there are many birds. These droppings, as well as any uneaten food, wash into your lake adding nutrients which encourage algal growth.

Ducks can often be seen paddling along the lakeshore.

Getting rid of ducks isn't always easy, either. They are more attracted by mowed lawns than by natural shoreline vegetation which might be hiding predators. You can remove Muscovy ducks but not wild ones, such as mallards, which are protected by law.

Those Without Backbones ("Bugs" and Others)

Ouch and Itch... Living at the lake, especially in Florida, means dealing with the insects which inhabit waterfront areas. A few tips may help you minimize their effects.

Mosquitoes. Many counties and municipalities spray regularly for mosquito control. However, you can reduce breeding sites by eliminating small standing water sources which serve as nurseries for mosquitoes. You can encourage natural predators such as bats, frogs, and birds. Electronic mosquito zappers probably will kill more beneficial insects than mosquitoes which are attracted by the carbon dioxide in your breath and body heat, not light. In addition to the personal repellents on the market, substances like citronella and pennyroyal have repellent ability.

Generally mosquitoes are more active in the evening; use repellent and/or protect yourself with long sleeves, pants, and a hat when they are numerous. In Florida, we have two forms of encephalitis carried by mosquitoes; timing your activity and dressing protectively will help avoid contracting this disease.

Deerflies. Luckily these are numerous only for short periods, but they do bite viciously. Choose insect repellents which deter these as well as mosquitoes.

"Chizziwinks." These non-biting midges (adult Chironomids) are also often called blind mosquitoes. Even though they won't bite you, they can be a real nuisance. They can hatch in such high densities that they can cause car accidents or allergic reactions in some people, cover houses, and stain paint.

Did you know...

Lake George and Lake Crescent have marine fish, such as striped mullet and American eel, as well as the usual freshwater fish because they are connected to the Atlantic Ocean through the St. Johns River.

Ticks. Deer ticks (which carry Lyme disease and also Erlichiosis) are smaller than the common dog tick. Only as big as a pinhead (or even smaller), they are not easy to see. They look a bit like freckles that walk! Wearing light clothing when going in wooded areas or tall grass, where they are most likely to occur, will make it easier to see them.

Check carefully for ticks after walks. Don't wear sandals or go barefoot in tall grass. Insect repellents containing DEET are effective, but should not be used heavily, especially on children. If you do find a tick attached, remove it with tweezers, trying not to squeeze its abdomen.

Not all deer ticks carry the spirochete bacteria which cause Lyme Disease. However, if you notice a rash, flu-like symptoms, or other suspicious symptoms after a tick bite, consult your doctor. The disease is not easy to diagnose and you may need to persist in seeking medical assistance. However, once diagnosed, it can be treated with antibiotics. Rapidly rising and falling body temperature could indicate Erlichiosis, another disease carried by ticks, which also responds well to antibiotics.

Fire Ants. If you live in Florida, you will soon become acquainted with the red fire ant (imported to the U.S. about 1940), which infests millions of acres in the South. Rounded conical nests can appear almost overnight in your lawn and other areas and need to be watched for.

They are easily encountered by children and pets, unaware of the danger. Fire ant stings are painful, may be slow to heal, and may become infected. Chemical treatment of individual mounds or the general area can control them. (See "For More Information" at the end of this chapter.)

Chiggers ("red bugs"). These very small larvae of mites attach themselves to your skin, causing itching and welts. Here in Florida, they are not known

*Ouch and Itch…
Living at the lake,
especially in Florida,
means dealing with the
insects which inhabit
waterfront areas.
A few tips may help you
minimize their effects.*

to transmit disease. However, the itching can be intense, causing scratching and possible infections as a result. They are often found in damp areas; however, they also are encountered in scrub areas with high rodent populations or your home lawn.

Chiggers often appear in patches which can be treated with insecticides (See "For More Information" at the end of this chapter); keeping lawns cut short also helps. Hot baths or showers with repeated soap scrubbing will remove them from your skin, but the welts may not be avoided. Try to prevent encounters by wearing protective clothing and applying repellents containing DEET (check for precautions on label and don't use on children).

"Itsy, bitsy spider..." In Florida, we grow 'em big. There are, of course, many small spiders, but we also have some big ones, such as the "banana spider" which grows to be several inches across. You may encounter them on their webs between trees if you are walking in the woods. While the spider will try to avoid you if you run into its web, there are startling moments while you check its whereabouts.

There are also poisonous spiders here, such as the black widow and the brown recluse, which may be encountered inside buildings. Once again, be alert and informed and learn to recognize those which are harmful.

What You Can't See...

Swimmer's Itch. Swimmers in a variety of lakes in Florida, as in northern lakes, may encounter "swimmer's itch". This is a skin rash

Did you know...

The canals which connect the Oklawaha Chain of Lakes (Lake and Orange Counties) were built back in the late 1800s for transportation. Roads were poor and both people and produce, including citrus and logging products, traveled through these canals.

which is an allergic reaction to an immature form of a parasitic worm which mistakenly burrows into human skin (then dies) instead of its usual waterfowl host. Showers followed by a good brisk toweling help to remove the animals before they can burrow.

Naegleria. More productive types of lakes ("green") may have a type of amoeba (*Naegleria fowleri*), a one-celled, microscopic animal which lives in lake bottoms, feeding on organic material in the sediments. Concentrations are rarely high enough to cause public health problems; however, increases can occur when waters are warm in late summer (July–October or November).

Swimmers may contact *Naegleria* when swimming along the lake bottom or jumping off docks stirring up bottom sediments. If the sediments contain the amoeba's mobile form, it can enter the brain through nasal passages and cause Primary Amoebic Meningoencephalitis (PAM). PAM is rare (1 case in 2.5 million exposures) — 15 deaths in Florida in the last 30 years — you should be aware of it, and see a doctor if illness occurs after swimming.

Mom, Can I Keep It?

For people living on the lakefront, especially in rural areas, this familiar question may be accompanied by the appearance of some type of wildlife. It may be a garter snake or a bullfrog, or it may be a baby raccoon or rabbit. Or it may be something you don't recognize. You may or may not want the child to keep it. However, it also may not be legal for you to possess, and it could possibly be harmful (for example, a poisonous snake).

The Florida Game and Fresh Water Fish Commission has regulations authorized by state law concerning the keeping and housing of both native and non-native animals.

The Florida Game and Fresh Water Fish Commission has regulations authorized by state law concerning the keeping and housing of both native and non-native animals. In general, you cannot keep either native or non-native wildlife in captivity without a permit[1]. A variety of laws at the

[1]39-6.0011 Fla. Administrative Code

federal, state, and local levels protect Florida's wildlife. (For a good introduction to these laws, see "Laws that Protect Florida's Wildlife" listed in "For More Information" at the end of this chapter.)

However, unless they are in a specific protected class (endangered, threatened, species of special concern, or exotic pest species) or regulated (alligators for example), you can keep some amphibians, reptiles, rabbits, rats, mice, hamsters, and gerbils[2]. You may not, however, keep a gopher tortoise (it is a protected species[3]) or a baby alligator.[4]

But what will happen to the baby animal you found if you don't care for it? It probably is not an orphan; the mother may be nearby. If it is, some species are very hard to raise. Baby rabbits rarely survive without the bacteria they get from their mother's fecal pellets. The cute baby raccoon may become a destructive pet as an adult.

Baby snakes do not always look like the adults, and a poisonous one may be mistaken for a harmless species. Try to become familiar with the wildlife in your area so you can identify the species you see. If you have a question regarding the status of a particular species, you can give your local Game and Fresh Water Fish Commission biologist a call (see Chapter 13 for map and phone numbers).

Introduced Exotic Pests

Those of you living in Florida, especially in South Florida, may very well run into exotic invaders. A variety of plants, invertebrates, amphibians, reptiles, birds, and mammals have been introduced and many are well established in our state.

But, what about the baby animal you found?

[2]39-6.0022 Fla. Administrative Code
[3]39-27.005 Fla. Administrative Code
[4]39-25.031 Fla. Administrative Code

While many introduced species of plants and animals have become a part of our landscape and cause no problems, some have become pests, either difficult to control or negatively impacting native species. A number of non-native aquatic plants, such as the water hyacinth, have been invaders of Florida aquatic systems for some time.

Marine toads, introduced in 1955 for insect control in sugar cane, are not uncommon in South Florida. These very large toads have adapted well and are often treated as backyard pets; however, they do have a negative impact on native amphibians. Also, pet dogs which bite the toads can become ill from poison in the toad's glands.

Aquarium owners dump plants and fish into lakes and rivers. Importers and pet owners allow amphibians and reptiles to escape. Tropical birds and mammals have escaped. Some species have been introduced for management reasons, such as grass carp brought in to help control aquatic plants.

Many introduced species of plants and animals have survived and are successfully breeding. Some, such as Oscars and Peacock bass, have become an excellent fishery in the South Florida canals. Others have become pests with detrimental effects on native organisms and lakes. Control of some of these species, such as the aquatic plants hydrilla and water hyacinth, is often difficult and expensive, costing the state millions of dollars each year.

Did you know...

Many lakes have islands but all islands are not the same. Some lakes, including, for example, Orange Lake in Alachua County, have floating islands, called tussocks. These are mats, sometimes very large, of floating vegetation which has become detached from the bottom and can move about, blocking access to bays and dock areas.

A few exotic pests:

- *Corbicula* — Asiatic Clam
- Tilapia
- Walking Catfish
- *Melaleuca*

- Brazilian pepper
- Water hyacinth
- *Hydrilla*

What you can do to prevent the spread of exotics:

- Clean your boat and trailer of plants and other aquatic organisms before you leave the ramp area.

- Be sure to drain wells and bilges before leaving the landing area.

- Wash your boat and trailer with hot water when you get home.

- Learn what the major exotic pest organisms look like. Report any new infestation to your local wildlife officer.

- Be sure to consult with your wildlife officer for advice and permits before you try to control exotic pests. Wrong control treatments can harm native plants and animals.

- Never dispose of aquarium fish or plants in native aquatic systems.

For More Information…

Wildlife

Chiggers.
  by P.G. Koehler. 1991. Institute of Food and Agricultural Sciences, University of Florida. Gainesville, Fla. Florida Cooperative Extension Service Fact Sheet ENY-212.
Controlling Pocket Gophers.
  by W.R. Marion. Institute of Food and Agricultural Sciences, University of Florida. Gainesville, Fla. Florida Cooperative Extension Service Fact Sheet FRC-35.
Dealing with Unwanted Wildlife in an Urban Environment.
  by Joe Schaefer. 1990. Institute of Food and Agricultural Sciences, University of Florida. Gainesville, Fla. Florida Cooperative Extension Service Fact Sheet SS-WIS-20.

Claude Brown

WARNING
HELP PREVENT THE SPREAD OF WATER WEED PROBLEMS PLEASE REMOVE PLANTS FROM TRAILERS BEFORE LEAVING THIS AREA THANK-YOU
SRWMD

Boaters can help stop the spread of exotic plants and animals by cleaning their boat trailers before leaving a boat landing.

Florida Frog Calls: A Guide to Commonly Heard Frogs and Toads.
  by R.A. Bradley. 1978. Florida State Museum, University of Florida. Gainesville, Fla.
  12" LP record.
Florida Wildlife. 1995. Beaver.
Florida Wildlife Code, Title 39.
  Florida Game and Fresh Water Fish Commission. 1995. Tallahassee, Fla. Revised regu-
  larly.
Handbook of Reptiles and Amphibians of Florida.
  by R.E. Ashton, Jr. and P.S. Ashton. 1988. Windward Pub. Co., Miami. Vol. I — The
  Snakes, Vol. II — The Turtles and Crocodilians, Vol. III — The Amphibians.
Imported Fire Ants.
  by P.G. Koehler. 1993. Institute of Food and Agricultural Sciences, University of Florida.
  Gainesville, Fla. Florida Cooperative Extension Service Fact Sheet ENY-226.
Imported Fire Ants and Their Management in Florida.
  1994. Institute of Food and Agricultural Sciences, University of Florida. Gainesville,
  Fla. Florida Cooperative Extension Service Fact Sheet SP-161. 24 pp.
Imported Fire Ants on Lawns and Turf.
  by D.H. Oi and P.G. Koehler. 1994. Institute of Food and Agricultural Sciences, Uni-
  versity of Florida. Gainesville, Fla. Florida Cooperative Extension Service Fact Sheet
  ENY-226.
Laws that Protect Florida's Wildlife.
  by Joe Schaefer and John Tucker. 1993. Institute of Food and Agricultural Sciences,
  University of Florida. Gainesville, Fla. Florida Cooperative Extension Service Fact Sheet
  SS-WIS-48.
Mosquitoes and Other Biting Flies.
  by P.G. Koehler. 1993. Institute of Food and Agricultural Sciences, University of Florida.
  Gainesville, Fla. Florida Cooperative Extension Service Fact Sheet ENY-220.
Southeastern Pocket Gopher.
  by W.H. Kern. Institute of Food and Agricultural Sciences, University of Florida.
  Gainesville, Fla. Florida Cooperative Extension Service Fact Sheet SS-WIS-67.
Status, pathway and time of introduction, present distribution, and significant ecological
  and economic effects.
  by James A. McCann, Lori N. Arkin, and James D. Williams. 1996. Published on the
  Internet, March 1996, by the University of Florida, Center for Aquatic Plants.
  National Biological Service, Southeastern Biological Science Center, 7920 N.W. 71st
  Street, Gaineville, Florida 32653 (http://aquat1.ifas.ufl.edu).
Stinging or Venomous Insects and Related Pests.
  by P.G. Koehler and D.E. Short. 1996. Institute of Food and Agricultural Sciences,
  University of Florida. Gainesville, Fla. Florida Cooperative Extension Service Fact Sheet
  ENY-215.
Structure-invading Ants of Florida.
  Institute of Food and Agricultural Sciences, University of Florida. Gainesville, Fla.
  Florida Cooperative Extension Service publication SP-164. 16 pp. ॐ

Mark V. Hoyer

Large wading birds often fish in the shallows of a sunny lakeshore.

CHAPTER 4

Aquatic Plants

…beautiful, beneficial, necessary, and nuisance.

Types of Aquatic Plants

All lakes have aquatic plants. Some aquatic plants are small, free-floating, and cannot be seen with the naked eye (algae), while others are large enough to be seen (macrophytes). The term aquatic macrophytes refers to a diverse group of aquatic plants encompassing flowering vascular plants, mosses, ferns, and macroalgae. Aquatic macrophytes provide habitat for fish and food for waterfowl. They also are the plants most often noticed by people who live on lakes and the ones that most often become problems.

As you look out over your lake from dry land to open water you will notice several types of aquatic macrophytes. This area, called the littoral zone, is defined as the area from the lake's edge to the maximum water depth where rooted plants will grow. There are four major groups of aquatic macrophytes in the littoral zone with which you should become familiar: emergent, floating-leaved, submersed, and free-floating.

Floating-leaved macrophytes are plants rooted to the lake bottom with leaves that float on the surface.

• • •

Free-floating macrophytes are a diverse group that typically float on or just under the water surface; they are not rooted to the bottom.

Emergent macrophytes grow on periodically inundated or submersed soils. Most emergent macrophytes are perennials (living three years or more). They are typically rooted in the lake bottom, have their base portions submersed, and have their tops elevated into the air. This is an ideal arrangement for plant growth. Nutrients are available from the sediment, water is available both in the sediment and overlying water, carbon dioxide is available from the air, and sunlight is not reduced by the water column. Common emergent macrophytes include plants such as maidencane or torpedograss (*Panicum* spp.), bulrushes (*Scirpus* spp.), cattails (*Typha* spp.), and spikerushes (*Eleocharis* spp.).

Floating-leaved macrophytes are plants rooted to the lake bottom with leaves that float on the surface. Common representatives include waterlilies (*Nymphaea* spp.), spatterdock (*Nuphar* spp.), and watershield (*Brasenia* spp.). Floating leaves are attached to roots or rhizomes with a flexible, tough stem. Many floating-leaved species — waterlilies for example — form large colonies from spreading underground rhizomes.

Submersed aquatic plants are those that grow completely underwater. These macrophytes are a diverse group that includes quillworts (*Isoetes* spp.), mosses (*Fontinalis* spp.), muskgrasses (*Chara* spp.), stoneworts (*Nitella* spp.), and numerous vascular plants. Many submersed plants, such as widgeon-grass (*Ruppia maritima*), various pondweeds (*Potamogeton* spp.), and tape-grass (*Vallisneria* spp.), are native to the United States. Others such as hydrilla (*Hydrilla verticillata*) are not native and are some of the worst aquatic nuisances.

Free-floating macrophytes are a diverse group that typically float on or just under the water surface; they are not rooted to the bottom. Small free-floating plants include duckweeds (*Lemna* spp.), mosquito fern (*Azolla caroliniana*), and water fern (*Salvinia* spp.). Larger surface-floating plants include water hyacinth (*Eichhornia crassipes*), frog's bit (*Limnobium spongia*), and water lettuce (*Pistia stratiotes*).

There are many species of aquatic plants and a variety of sources of information available to help you identify them. In addition to manuals designed for field identification, there is information, including videos, produced and distributed by the University of Florida's Center for Aquatic Plants, which will help you identify and become acquainted with the common macrophytes in Florida. Also, the Florida Plant Management Society has information available, including a laminated identification chart (see references at the end of this section).

Biology of Aquatic Plants

Many factors determine the distribution and abundance of aquatic macrophytes in your lake. These factors include but are not limited to: light availability, nutrient concentration (primarily phosphorus and nitrogen) and general water chemistry, substrate characteristics, and the size and shape of your lake. If all of these factors are favorable, aquatic macrophytes can become extremely abundant.

While environmental characteristics can determine the distribution and abundance of aquatic macrophytes, the plants themselves also can influence many environmental and biologi-

Did you know...

Most Florida lakes are sinkhole lakes, formed by erosion of the underlying limestone, which collapsed, forming the lake. They may lie in "sinkhole depressions" and may be circular in shape. North Florida and Central Florida are dotted with circular lakes.

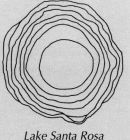

Lake Santa Rosa

Adapted from E.E. Shannon and P.L. Brezonik, 1972, Limnological Characteristics of North and Central Florida Lakes, Limnol. Oceanogr. 17:97-110

cal interactions in your lake. At this point we will discuss only a few of these interactions to help you understand the role these plants may play in your lake and help you determine how you want to manage the aquatic macrophytes which are there.

As water moves through macrophyte beds, water turbulence is reduced, allowing fine particles to settle out within the plant bed. These beds also act as a sieve, retaining coarse particles of organic material as well. Beds of plants also protect the shore from erosion by wind-driven waves or currents. If you watch your lake on a windy day, you will notice that the water is calmer in the plant beds compared to the open water or bare shorelines. Both of these mechanisms increase the accumulation of sediments, usually undesirable to people who like to swim or wade at the water's edge.

Aquatic macrophytes have an inverse relationship with water clarity. As aquatic macrophyte abundance increases in a lake, the amount of suspended algae, the primary determinant of water clarity in most lakes, decreases. There are several hypotheses which may explain this inverse relationship. One suggests that aquatic plants and the attached algae compete for the nutrients that would otherwise be used to produce suspended algae. Another hypothesis suggests that aquatic plants stabilize sediments and reduce the resuspension of nutrients that could be used by suspended algae. Regardless of which of these or other mechanisms, working independently or together, cause this inverse relationship, the fact that it exists has been documented many times.

The inverse relationship between aquatic plants and water clarity needs to be discussed when planning any aquatic plant management because the control of abundant aquatic plants to alleviate one defined problem may cause another perceived problem. Most people consider clear water very desirable in their lake. When clarity decreases from 15 feet to 3 feet after an

Algae under the microscope

aquatic plant control project, people may decide that the aquatic plant problem was not as bad as the reduced water clarity which followed. This usually will not occur when aquatic plants covering less than 30% of the lake's surface area are removed or reduced. However, your lake's water clarity will most likely decrease after aquatic plants covering more than 50% of the lake surface area are controlled.

Dissolved oxygen levels may vary a great deal over a 24-hour period in waters of dense submersed macrophyte stands. During daylight hours, while photosynthesis occurs, water can become supersaturated with oxygen. Respiration by the plants and other organisms at night, however, can deplete dissolved oxygen in dense beds with little water circulation. Dense growths of floating or matted submersed species also reduce oxygen levels by inhibiting oxygen exchange with the atmosphere. Thus, oxygen depletion occurring within extensive mats of aquatic macrophytes can be enough to contribute to fish kills in your lake.

The frequency of oxygen loss and many other interactions between fish and aquatic plants are highly variable, which makes it difficult to generalize. Relationships vary because of differences in aquatic systems, plant forms and abundances, fish species composition, and geographic area. However, there are fish species whose abundance usually increases (such as blue-spotted sunfish), decreases (such as gizzard shad), or does not change (largemouth bass) as aquatic macrophytes increase in a lake.

A major factor determining the value of aquatic plants to a particular fish species is whether the fish is prey for another species or is predatory. The presence of aquatic macrophytes increases the structural complexity of lake ecosystems, providing refuges for prey and interfering with the feeding of some predators. As you might expect, feeding behavior in small fish is

A major factor determining the value of aquatic plants to a particular fish species is whether the fish is prey for another species or is predatory.

strongly influenced by their exposure to predators. If they are relatively safe from predators (and not constantly watching for danger) they can forage more effectively. For large predators, the visual barriers of plant stems decrease foraging efficiency; so they grow more slowly in habitats with more structure.

These are only a few of the important relationships that exist between aquatic plants and fish populations. Unfortunately, these relationships give little insight into how aquatic macrophytes affect "fishing." Some anglers enjoy fishing in aquatic plant beds and some do not, but most anglers agree that there can be too many aquatic plants for good fishing.

So, how many plants do we need to provide habitat for fish populations and "structure" for anglers ("weed" beds, stumps, fallen logs, and shallow areas which attract fish and tell you where the big one is). Too few plants generally do not provide enough cover; too many may lead to stunted fish populations, poor predator growth, fish kills, and poor fishing. The answer then is a moderate amount of aquatic plants. Several studies have suggested optimum vegetative coverages for healthy fish populations ranging from 15–85%. It is important to note, however, that lakes with no aquatic plants and those completely covered with aquatic plants will both support fish populations. The problem is that some fish do not occur in the desired abundance.

Similar to interactions between aquatic macrophytes and fish, those between aquatic birds, other wildlife, and aquatic plants are also highly variable. These relationships vary because of differences in aquatic systems, plant forms and abundances, bird species composition, and geographic area. Generally, however, there are groups of bird species that increase in abundance (ring-necked duck for example); others decrease in abundance (such as double-crested cormorant) as aquatic macrophyte abundance increases in a lake.

Submerged aquatic plants are good cover for game fish.

Joe Richard

Lake Baldwin: A Management Success Story?

Sometimes a successful lake management story has an ending that not everyone likes. Consider the case of Lake Baldwin.

Lake Baldwin is a 200-acre lake located at the U.S Naval Training Center in Orlando, Florida. The lake is used primarily for swimming, general boating, and fishing. An exotic submersed plant, called hydrilla, became established in the lake some time around 1971. By the middle to late 1970s, Lake Baldwin was almost completely covered with this exotic plant. The hydrilla made it almost impossible to use the lake for swimming, boating, or fishing. So, grass carp were added to control the hydrilla. From 1975 to 1978, over 2500 grass carp were stocked; by 1981, all aquatic plants were gone from Lake Baldwin.

This is a success story because people can once again use Lake Baldwin for recreational activities. However, during the years with hydrilla, the water was crystal clear allowing visibility to approximately 15 feet. Because hydrilla used the available nutrients, there were no algal blooms to cloud the water. After the grass carp ate the hydrilla, lake water clarity decreased to about 5 feet. Therefore, while the aquatic weeds were successfully controlled, some people were not prepared for the loss of their crystal clear water.

Ken Langeland

Lake Baldwin before

Mark V. Hoyer

Lake Baldwin after

When are Aquatic Plants a Problem?

All aquatic plants (native and introduced) have the potential to become a problem. If a plant interferes with a particular use of a lake then its presence is a problem; if it enhances that use then it is beneficial. Whether native or introduced, how aquatic macrophytes affect your lake depends on the planned uses of that lake. Because lakes cannot be all things to all people, even the macrophyte abundance within a given lake can be positive or negative depending on one's use of the lake. Thus, defining the primary uses of a lake is the first step when determining if there is an aquatic weed problem.

It is probably safe to say that no two people see exactly the same things when they assess a lake. Long-term residents who have witnessed hydrilla mats come and go will probably react very differently from new arrivals to the neighborhood who have never seen the dramatic changes that can occur as hydrilla fills the water column of a lake. The loudest voices at the homeowners' association meeting may be from the members unable to remember how extensive the cattails were before the dredging project was undertaken. Others may simply have spent little time around water before and don't have the experience to separate a serious problem from a normal occurrence.

To further complicate the situation, things that look like problems may not be, and seriously degraded conditions may not attract any attention at all. We humans are extremely visually oriented, and easily impressed by rather small changes in large items. Doubling of cattail

Did you know...

The water in darkwater lakes, such as the Alligator Chain in Osceola County, is stained by water received from poorly drained soils such as cypress swamps. With time the color bleaches out. So, when water flows through a chain of lakes, the color (stain) tends to decrease as the water flows downstream.

coverage from four to eight acres over a two-year period may mean something dramatic is happening to water depth (is sediment filling in the bottom?), or the plant may be re-invading following last year's mechanical removal project. Regardless, the expansion of cattail will probably be noticed by many, unlike the more subtle and probably far more important changes that may be taking place in the water chemistry of the lake. Reliable historical information, collected in an appropriate manner by knowledgeable people, can do more than almost anything else to resolve discussions of "what is happening to the lake?" A water quality or aquatic macrophyte monitoring system like the citizen volunteer programs in New Hampshire, Vermont, Wisconsin, and here in Florida can yield valuable information to help guide lake management decisions.

Three species of aquatic macrophytes have been particularly troublesome in Florida. Water hyacinth, hydrilla, and water lettuce have been the objects of extensive research and control programs throughout Florida.

Water Hyacinth (Eichhornia crassipes). This is a free-floating plant that was introduced to Florida. Water hyacinth has long leathery leaves and showy flowers and can grow to a meter in height. It floats and thus is moved around through wind and currents; however, it will root in backwater shallows. It is often confused with frog's bit (*Limnobium spongia*), a native plant, when seen from a distance. One of frog's bit's two types of leaves resembles the leathery leaves of the water hyacinth. However, the hyacinth has spikes of showy lavender or violet flowers; frog's bit has white flowers which are not showy.

Water hyacinth reproduces rapidly, both vegetatively by "runner" and by seeds which can repopulate an area after a drought. Control of this plant has cost the State of Florida millions of dollars but has been successful. The Bureau of Aquatic Plant Management, a division of the Department of

… knowledgeable people, can do more than almost anything else to resolve discussions of "what is happening to the lake?"

Environmental Protection (DEP), reports a ten-fold reduction of lake surface coverage from 1983–1993.

Hydrilla (Hydrilla verticillata). Hydrilla (Florida elodea) is an introduced exotic which has been difficult to control. Despite efforts to control hydrilla, the infested acreage in Florida waters doubled between 1983 and 1985. The long, branched stems break, forming new plants which make floating mats. It has several methods of reproduction, including winter buds (turions) and tubers, which allow it to survive cold winters and drought. It looks similar to Brazilian elodea but feels rough when drawn through the hand whereas Brazilian elodea feels smooth.

Water Lettuce (Pistia stratiotes). This plant (probably introduced) looks like an open head of lettuce floating on the water. Like water hyacinth, it reproduces rapidly. Because the plants float loosely, wind can move them into traffic areas, clogging canals and interfering with navigation. Water lettuce has little value for wildlife, although small aquatic animals find it useful as a nesting area. An active control program for water lettuce has resulted in cutting the number of acres covered in half over the ten-year period from 1983–1993.

Aquatic Plant Management

What are some of the problems that these and other aquatic plants can cause in your lake? Aquatic macrophytes can:

1)   Increase organic sedimentation filling in canals and lake bottoms with decomposing organic matter.

2)   Physically block lake entrances or boat movement on the lake with living or dead and floating plants. The blockages can also restrict

Dense macrophyte growth separates this home from open water.

Mark V. Hoyer

water movement, causing either flooding or drought depending on which side of the blockage you are.

3) Cause problems that range from minor to severe for swimmers, water skiers, and other recreational water users.

4) Provide a refuge for mosquitoes linked to diseases such as equine encephalitis. They also harbor organisms (snails, clams, and worms) required for the life cycle of trematodes that can cause "swimmers itch."

5) Cause severe oxygen depletion killing many organisms that live in a lake, including fish.

If you think your lake has an aquatic plant problem, first determine what federal, state, or local agencies are responsible for aquatic plant management in that lake. The agencies, starting with DEP, should then be contacted to determine what assistance is available and what an individual can legally do on his or her own. Problems on public lakes, which affect the public's access and use of the lake, will normally be the responsibility of a public agency. Decisions concerning perceived whole-lake problems on private lakes should be addressed through consensus of a homeowners' association after obtaining recommendations from public agencies.

Problems affecting your lake as a whole are normally managed by a public agency or a commercial aquatic plant management firm with the necessary equipment and expertise. Management of aquatic vegetation in small areas along private beaches or around boat docks may be accomplished by the individual property owner, although even in these situations it usually is best to obtain the services of an experienced aquatic plant manager.

If you think your lake has an aquatic plant problem, first determine what federal, state, or local agencies are responsible for aquatic plant management in that lake.

If you decide to conduct your own aquatic plant management you need to know first what can be done legally. Before you consider removing aquatic plants from your shoreline or lake, you may need to obtain a permit from the Department of Environmental Protection. (Permits are no longer required for vegetation and muck removal involving less than 50 feet or 50% of the shoreline (whichever is greater). Contact your regional office of the Bureau for Aquatic Plant Management for assistance (see Chapter 13). You should also check with your municipality and/or county. Many have environmental codes and may also require a permit. If herbicides are planned, use only those registered for use in aquatic sites and become fully trained in their use. Don't rely on your neighbor's experience; there have been recent changes in state law relative to shoreline alteration, vegetation clearing, and aquatic plant control; and more and more local codes are in existence.

Aquatic Plant Control

The diversity of lake types and expectations of water resource users demand that commercial and public aquatic plant managers, as well as individual waterfront property owners, carefully choose the most appropriate method or combination of methods to manage aquatic plants for each individual situation. Methods that may be considered for managing aquatic plants include physical removal, habitat alteration, biological controls, and herbicides. Each method has its own effectiveness, cost, and impact on the lake system as well as lake uses.

Physical removal of aquatic plants can range from the hand removal of a few square feet next to a dock, to mechanical harvesting of several acres of boat lanes. Generally, physical removal of aquatic plants is effective but of short duration because plants can grow back rapidly. Thus, physical removal of aquatic plants is an ongoing control technique, much as mowing your

Before you consider removing aquatic plants from your shoreline or lake, you may need to obtain a permit from the Department of Environmental Protection…

lawn in the Florida summer. Physical removal of plants is also expensive because after you remove the plants from the lake you have to put them somewhere. Aquatic plants are approximately 95% water; it requires a lot of energy to move plants that are made up of mostly water, which weighs in at 8 pounds per gallon! So this technique is better suited for spot treatments in lakes and not whole-lake management.

Habitat alterations range from dredging a canal to a depth where aquatic plants cannot grow to changing the water level of a whole lake to control or encourage certain species of plants. These can be effective and long-term aquatic plant management activities but require a great deal of planning to accomplish. This approach can be inexpensive if control structures already exist and expensive if water control structures have to be built or water has to be pumped.

The use of herbicides to control aquatic plants can range from spot-treating cattails around a dock to whole lake treatments to control hydrilla. Herbicide treatments can be effective but are relatively short term (one to two years of control) and usually have to be repeated. Any use of chemicals (herbicides) to control aquatic plants requires a permit from the Department of Environmental Protection. Herbicides differ in their effectiveness; dosage rates need to be carefully determined; and application techniques require training. If this is an appropriate solution to your aquatic plant problem, you may need to hire someone who

Did you know…

Florida's many springs, such as those at Manatee State Park and Silver Springs have a constant temperature of about 72° F. (This is the groundwater temperature in North and North Central Florida). Swimming in these springs can be a cooling summer experience! Some of these springs have a tremendous flow of water. For example, Silver Springs has a flow volume of more than 550 million gallons of water per day.

is licensed to use chemical control. There is a real potential for harming the lake or your water supply should chemical control be done incorrectly.

Biological control of aquatic plants can range from stocking insects to control alligator weed to stocking fish to eat hydrilla. The most common biological control of aquatic plants with which you will come in contact is the use of grass carp. These are fish which primarily eat plants. Florida requires the use of triploid grass carp which cannot reproduce, and a permit is required before you can add them to your lake. The Florida Game and Fresh Water Fish Commission is in charge of grass carp permits and can be contacted for information and advice on how and whether to proceed with this method (see Chapter 13).

If stocked at a high enough density, grass carp can be very effective and inexpensive in removing aquatic vegetation. However, you need to be aware that the grass carp have the potential to eat all the aquatic vegetation in your lake! Thus, you should only use grass carp when the complete control of aquatic vegetation is an acceptable management objective.

You can see that there are many methods of aquatic plant control and that the science of aquatic plant management is a complicated business. Before you begin controlling aquatic plants, you should formulate an aquatic plant management plan with the help of aquatic plant experts. Contacting the DEP Bureau of Aquatic Plant Management would be a good place start to find help in developing an aquatic plant management plan. Another good source of information is the newly available manual "Aquatic Plant Management in Lakes and Reservoirs" by Hoyer et al. (see below).

Before you begin controlling aquatic plants, you should formulate an aquatic plant management plan with the help of aquatic plant experts.

From Lake to Prairie and Back Again?

Paynes Prairie, south of Gainesville, was once known as Lake Alachua. In the 1890s, steamboats ferried people and goods across the lake. When the water level went down during the years , it apparently dropped so rapidly that the boats were left stranded; the hulks were visible for years after. Now called Paynes Prairie State Park, the area serves as home to a variety of wildlife, including many alligators, especially near the area known as the "Alachua Sink." High rainfall levels in 1997-98 filled the prairie to such an extent that the view from US 441, which cuts directly across the prairie, was a panorama of shimmering water rather than a prairie full of grasses and trees. This very wet year came after 30 years of below-normal rainfall, and many lakes rose, sometimes reclaiming areas that hadn't been covered with water for many years. To the surprise of some homeowners, their subdivision homes became lakefront homes, or in the worst cases, submersed fish habitats! Taking a long-term view in investigating the history of your prospective lakefront home might help you plan your homesite for high water possibilities and avoid sites which have flood histories.

Paynes Prairie State Park at both low and high water levels. (Photos compliments of the Florida Department of Environmental Protection, Paynes Prairie State Park)

For More Information...

You can obtain further information on specific plants, their biology and control by
contacting: Aquatic Plant Information Retrieval System
        Aquatic Plant Center, University of Florida
        7922 NW 71st St.
        Gainesville, FL 32653
        World Wide Web: http://aquat1.ifas.ufl.edu/

Aquascaping Freshwater Ecosystems.
    by Will Miller. *LakeLine*, March, 1988:4.

Aquascaping: Planting and Maintenance.
    by D. Butts, J. Hinton, C. Watson, K. Langeland, D. Hall, and M. Kane. Institute of Food
    and Agricultural Sciences, University of Florida. Gainesville, Fla. Florida Cooperative Ex-
    tension Service Circular 912.

Aquatic and Wetland Plant Identification Manual.
    Department of Environmental Protection, Bureau of Aquatic Plant Management, Divi-
    sion of Resource Management. Tallahassee, Fla. 35303.

Aquatic and Wetland Plant Identification Series.
    Institute for Food and Agricultural Sciences, University of Florida. Gainesville, Fla. Florida
    Cooperative Extension Service videotapes SM-361, 369, 360, 363, 371, 362, and 370.
    This seven-tape series features some of the most common or important aquatic and
    wetland plants in Florida. Recommended for the general public, the information in these
    tapes is presented in everyday language.

Aquatic Pest Control Training Manual.
    Institute for Food and Agricultural Sciences, University of Florida. Gainesville, Fla. Florida
    Cooperative Extension Service publication SM-2. 107 pp.

Aquatic Plant Identification Deck.
    Center for Aquatic Plants. Institute for Food and Agricultural Sciences, University of Florida.
    Gainesville, Fla. Florida Cooperative Extension Service publication SM-50. 72 cards. A
    "deck of cards" with color pictures and descriptive information. The plants are indexed
    by both scientific and common names.

Aquatic Plant Management in Lakes and Reservoirs.
    M.V. Hoyer and D.E. Canfield, Jr., eds. 1997. Prepared by the North American Lake Man-
    agement Society (P.O. Box 5443 Madison WI 53705) and the Aquatic Plant Manage-
    ment Society (P.O. Box 1477, Lehigh FL 33970) for US EPA, Washington DC.

Aquatic Weed Management Guide.
    Institute for Food and Agricultural Sciences, University of Florida. Gainesville, Fla. Florida
    Cooperative Extenson Service publication SP-55. 102 pp.

Florida Aquatic Plant Survey Report.
    by J.D. Schardt and J.A. Ludlow. 1993. Bureau of Aquatic Plant Management, Depart-
    ment of Environmental Protection. Tallahassee, Fla.

Florida's Aquatic Plant Story.
    Institute for Food and Agricultural Sciences, University of Florida. Gainesville, Fla. Florida

Many macrophytes have showy flower stalks and look beautiful along the water's edge.

Vic Ramey

Cooperative Extension Service videotape SV-315. 24 min.

Florida Freshwater Plants: A Handbook of Common Aquatic Plants in Florida Lakes.
by M.V. Hoyer, D.E. Canfield, Jr., C.A. Horsburgh, and K. P. Brown. 1996. Institute for Food and Agricultural Sciences, University of Florida. Gainesville, Fla. Florida Cooperative Extension Service publication SP-189. 264 pp.

Hydrilla: A Continuing Problem in Florida Waters.
by K.A. Langeland. 1990. Institute for Food and Agricultural Sciences, University of Florida. Gainesville, Fla. Florida Cooperative Extension Service Circular 884.

Identification Manual for Wetland Plants.
Institute for Food and Agricultural Sciences, University of Florida. Gainesville, Fla. Florida Cooperative Extension Service publication SP- 35. 297 pp.

Weeds in the Sunshine: Information for Control of Florida Weeds.
Institute of Food and Agricultural Sciences, University of Florida. Gainesville, Fla. Florida Cooperative Extension Service Fact Sheets SS-AGR-01 through SS-AGR-52.

Commercial Sources for Native Aquatic Plants

Aurora Incorporated.
Ellenton.

Central Florida Native Flora, Inc.
PO Box 1045
San Antonio, FL 33576
Tel. (904) 588-3687

Florida Natives Nursery, Inc.
5121 Ehrlich Rd.
Tampa, FL 33624
Tel. (407) 264-5765

Hollie's Farm and Garden, Florida Native Tree Farm
357 County Line Rd.
Lutz, FL 33549
Tel. (407) 949-6735

The Locator. Florida Dept. of Agriculture and Consumer Services (This publication lists specific plants and Florida businesses which supply aquatic plants.)
Bureau of Seafood and Aquaculture
2051 E Dirac Dr.
Tallahassee, FL 32310

Plant and Service Directory. Association of Florida Native Plant Nurseries.
AFNN
PO Box 434
Melrose, FL 32666
Tel. (352) 475-5513 or 1-800-293-5513

Floating macrophytes can fill up channels and ramps thus blocking boat traffic.

Noxious and Poisonous Plants

...if you see them, let them be.

"Leaves of three, let it be" is the old adage. Poison ivy is commonly encountered in Florida as well as many other parts of the United States. The presence of three leaves should alert you that the plant may be poison ivy and should be left alone.

Learn to identify the plant when you see it. However, both the leaf shape and the plant are highly variable. The edges may be more or less jagged (toothed) and the plant may be several inches high or a vine going up a tree, its huge leaves mingling with those of the tree. It may be found growing at the base of trees, radiating out from the base (apparently started by bird droppings), mingled in among the grass in open woods, or growing along roadsides and disturbed edges of wooded areas.

We are all familiar with the red, itchy, sometimes watery swellings resulting from contact with poison ivy. (Not everyone is sensitive to it and your sensitivity can change over time.) Oils from any part of the plant can produce this reaction, including the roots. Digging with your hands among its roots if it is in your garden, or even handling your garden hoe or trowel can get the oil of the plant on your skin. Wearing gloves when gardening is a good idea for many reasons, including avoiding poison ivy. Don't try to pull it out by hand, and never burn it. The oils are carried in the smoke as an aerosol.

Your local garden store can provide you with chemical sprays which can eradicate poison ivy. You will have to be persistent and spray again later, if it comes back, until the whole system is gone.

"Leaves of three, let it be" is the old adage.

• • •

Learn to identify the plant when you see it.

You may also encounter poison sumac, which grows as a shrub or small tree in boggy areas or near the edge of lakes. It produces drooping clusters of whitish berry-like fruits and has compound leaves (7–13 leaflets, frequently turned upward). Seedlings have 3 leaflets. Skin reaction, precautions, and control are similar to those for poison ivy.

In south Florida and the Keys, poison-wood (coral-sumac) may be encountered. This is a woody shrub or small tree with milky juice in the bark which upon contact produces symptoms similar to poison ivy. It has compound leaves with 5–7 oval, leathery leaflets (no teeth).

Other Poisonous Plants. Plants can be toxic to humans and animals in a number of ways. Some produce reactions upon contact with the skin, others upon ingestion. Toxicity can depend upon factors such as the part of the plant, the season and the differing reactions between individuals.

Poison Ivy is identifiable by its three-leaf structure.

Many species of plants which are poisonous or toxic to some degree grow here in Florida. Some are native and others often used as landscape plants. You should be familiar with them, especially if you have young children or pets who may eat or chew on the leaves. Oleander is one example. Angel's trumpet (a type of Jimson Weed), a member of the nightshade family, is another.

There are a number of good books available on poisonous plants; having one handy is a good idea.

For More Information…

Poisonous Plants of the Southern U.S.
    by John W. Everest, Thomas A. Powe, Jr., and John D. Freeman. 1996. Institute of Food and Agricultural Sciences, University of Florida. Gainesville,Fla. Florida Co-operative Extension Service publication SP-57. 30 pp. ❧

Sal Salazar

CHAPTER 5

Fulfilling Your Dream: How to Select and Develop a Lakeside Property

For those of you who now own lakefront property, the choice has already been made. Perhaps you have completed development of your property; or maybe you are in the process of deciding between natural and landscaped areas, putting in or repairing docks and storage buildings, or working on the shoreline. This process can enhance the value and usefulness of the property to you; it can also have either protective or damaging effects on your lake.

If you are prospective owners of lakefront property, making the right choice can make the difference between a dream fulfilled and a disappointment. We hope this chapter and the two which follow will be useful to all of you in the process of selecting, developing, and maintaining your lakefront property.

The Right Choice

If you are considering buying lakefront property, ask yourself some questions first. Will this be your primary residence or a second home; will you live

there part of the year or come on weekends? If weekends, how far would you want to drive? If this will be your primary residence and you have children, you will need to consider schools and other activities. Is the extra cost associated with lakefront property worth it to you relative to other expenses? You should be aware that, in general, lakefront property is considerably more expensive than comparable property not on the water. Also, your bank or mortgage company may require you to take out flood insurance. Thinking about these questions before you search and especially before you buy or build, may prevent choices that are inappropriate for your needs.

How do you go about choosing lakefront property?

How do you go about choosing lakefront property? Many of the factors which should be weighed are the same as those which would be important in buying property not on water. Location relative to conveniences, quality and distance of schools, and price relative to property values are always important factors. For example, look at the houses around the prospective property to see if they are at least of comparable value. Talk to local realtors about prospective neighborhoods, and discuss how they might fit your needs and interests.

Lakefront property involves other considerations. Does the water level fluctuate, for example, due to drawdowns? The pretty bay you are looking at in the spring may be a muddy, marshy area by summer where your boat will not float. Look at the aquatic vegetation. This can tell you something about water level fluctuations and substrates.

Is the property on the lee or windward side of the lake? Windy shores might mean boats must be pulled out or anchored offshore. This may also determine whether you can or could have a sandy beach. If the property is wooded, which direction does the property face? Will you have morning sun and afternoon shade or the reverse? This might be important to you.

Check to see whether the property is likely to be wet or tends to flooding. You can often tell by the vegetation or wildlife. For example, gopher tortoise burrows usually mean the land is higher and less likely to be wet. Cattails and sedges far up into the property from the shore tell you that it is probably wet at least sometimes. The presence of cypress knees in your yard also tells you that the area has been wet. Ask the neighbors about any recent floods or water level changes.

Look around and see how your prospective neighbors use the lake. Do you see motorboats and personal watercraft at the docks, or sailboats and canoes? Are there swimming beaches? In other words, try to see if your interests are compatible with existing uses; if they are very different, either you or the neighbors may be unhappy.

What About Zoning?

You will need to check to see if there are laws which might impact the type of use you want to make of your new property. Zoning may determine what and where you can build and otherwise impact your use of the property or lake. If the property you are interested in is on a small or no-wake lake and your interests are in waterskiing or jetskiing, it is not a good choice.

Look around at the lake, the other properties, and what type of recreational activities and boats others have. If you would be the only one with fast boats or jet skis, there may be laws which regulate or prevent their use on this lake or it may be too small. Be sure to get a survey before you buy if one has not been done. The mortgage company will probably require one anyway. This will protect you from finding out that your neighbor's outbuilding, fence or driveway is on your property (or the reverse) and help to prevent eventual problems with the neighbors.

Large lakes usually mean motor boat traffic.

Jet-skis are fun but may be disruptive.

Become familiar with the lake to discover if it fits your needs. Lakes are not all equal! Chapters 2–4 explained lake characteristics, how lakes function, and how to decide which lake is right for you.

Developing Your Property

Now that you are the owner of lakefront property, the real work begins! If you have purchased an existing home, your property may already be well-developed and maintained, and you only need to keep it that way. If it is undeveloped, building your home, and all the things that go with it, including landscaping and shoreline care will take careful planning, both for your sake and for your lake. The next sections offer you some helpful ideas ranging from building your home to putting in docks, caring for lawns and natural areas to aquascaping your shoreline.

Things to Consider Before You Buy…

- ✔ Your lifestyle
- ✔ Location (resale value, location of conveniences, stores, schools)
- ✔ Zoning
- ✔ Existence of a survey
- ✔ Lake type and quality (relative to your needs)

Building Your Lakefront Home

> *…to build your house on the shore of a lake*
> *means care in decisions and choices you make.*

Whether you find a piece of property with an existing home, or plan to build your home on the lake, check the local zoning regulations that protect lakeshores and/or water (see chapters 4 and 5). Are there available building sites and, if needed, septic field sites which conform with regulations?

Now that you are the owner of lakefront property, the real work begins!

Siting. Look at your property carefully as you consider what final look you would like to have. If a natural setting is your goal, look for landscape features which can be of advantage to you. What view of the lake will you get from particular places in the house. How will the house look from the water? Do you want it hidden from view, fitting into the natural vegetation with as little disturbance as possible? Look at the house orientation with regard to solar energy. Proper orientation can reduce your cooling costs.

Plan your driveway or road to avoid disturbing native vegetation. Consider shade, aesthetic, and economic values of existing trees before removing them. It is easier to remove them later than to regret their loss. Your county or town may have maps which can tell you about surface and ground-water flow directions. This can help place the house to avoid flooding and to get proper drain field placement for your septic system.

Contractors. If this is a new area for you, finding a good contractor may take a bit of searching. You can get lists of local contractors from Chambers of Commerce, builders associations, realtors, banks, etc. Asking neighbors or owners of houses you particularly like about their builders is especially useful; having a contractor who has worked on lakefront property and is willing to try to minimize disturbance and vegetation loss is easier for you and protective of the lake.

Once you have a particular contractor in mind, things to check are basically the

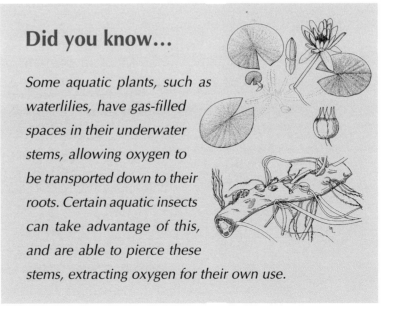

Did you know...

Some aquatic plants, such as waterlilies, have gas-filled spaces in their underwater stems, allowing oxygen to be transported down to their roots. Certain aquatic insects can take advantage of this, and are able to pierce these stems, extracting oxygen for their own use.

same as for any home building project. These include experience, quality of workmanship, education and certification, reputation, warranty, references, and probable subcontractors. Check the references and look at houses the contractor has built. Were they well-made and done on schedule? The contractor's personality is also important — you have to work closely with this person and want a positive experience.

Choice of Materials. Choice of building materials is generally a matter of personal choice and style of house being built. However, in Florida, the effects of heat and humidity must be considered. Rot-resistant wood, sun-resistant materials and paint, and proper termite protection are essential.

Reducing Rot. Designing with an eye to preventing damage from humidity and moisture is important in Florida. Keeping wood away from soil, a good roof overhang (preferably 2 feet), using flashing at horizontal joints where materials change, rust-proof nails, mildewcided and/or treated wood and termite protection procedures are all important in building for a longer home life.

When landscaping, remember that while shade is important in energy conservation, shading also reduces drying when wood gets wet or damp. Vegetation against a building reduces air circulation on the face of the siding. Remove pine needles and other debris from roofs, even shingles can break down faster if wet continuously. Keeping indoor humidity low through air conditioning and exhaust vents will prevent damage due to condensation of moisture. (See "Design Consideration for Wooden Structures in Florida" listed under "For More Information" at the end of this chapter.)

Preventing Construction Damage. Discuss the area to be cleared before construction begins. Contractors differ in their attitudes about working

Thomas Wright

Lakefront landscaping can be formal or informal depending on the owner's tastes.

around trees on the building site. One person went to see his beautiful wooded building site to find the whole site cleared. The site he had bought because of its many trees was now bare! The contractor preferred cleared sites.

An understanding should be reached between you and your contractor about what is to cleared, and what should be protected. Fencing special trees will keep equipment away from them and prevent damage to roots from compaction. Pines to be saved must be protected from damage; injured trees may die later or be good targets for Southern Pine Beetles. Damaged limbs should be removed.

Looking Your Best. How your place looks from the lake may also be important to you. Consider the view from the lake when siting the house and planning accessory buildings and docks. There may be restrictions on construction on the water's edge. (Check zoning regulations, see Section 2 for agencies).

What do you see when you view your lakefront home from the lake? You may want it to look as natural as possible, blending with the landscape. Maybe you want to encourage wildlife or just reduce yard work by keeping as much of your property as natural as possible. Consider placing shades on one side of your outdoor lights to reduce their impact on views from the lake or your neighbor's house.

Your House and Extended Absences. Whether you leave for the summer or go for an extended vacation during the winter, there are certain things which you may want to do. The time of year, where you live in Florida, and the length of time you will be gone will determine what you do about utilities, AC, heat, and water. Leaving your air conditioner on during your summer absence will prevent the buildup of humidity inside your home. Alternatively,

Consider the view from the lake when siting the house and planning accessory buildings and docks.

you may want to equip your air conditioner with a timer and run it for two hours in the very early morning, setting it low enough to run continuously during that period.

Leaving heat on during winter absences will avoid frozen water pipes during an unexpected freeze. (Draining water pipes during an extended winter absence is probably safest.) However, an extended electrical outage could cause trouble. It is a good idea to have someone check regularly on your home with emergency instructions. (See "Closing your Florida Home" listed under "For More Information" at the end of this chapter for helpful tips on preventing problems while you are away.)

Your Home Sewage System

Those of you who are already lakefront property owners and are not within a city or municipality probably have your own sewage disposal system. Do you know where it is and how well it is functioning? Keeping your system working properly is important to both you and your lake. Obviously, a failing system can be a health hazard, but poorly functioning systems can be detrimental to your lake, adding nutrients and encouraging algal or aquatic plant growth. A system constructed to meet today's standards, however, does a good job of treating sewage.

If you are considering buying, the lake property may be in a rural area and you will have or need to install your own sewage

Did you know...

Have you ever noticed smooth areas, sometimes in streaks, on a lake on a windy day? These are called "slicks" and are caused by oil produced by the normal activities of aquatic plants and animals. When wind ripples the lake surface, the oil in the "slick" area prevents ripples in that area. This thin layer of oil reduces surface tension and prevents the wavelets from forming. These smooth areas are the streaks that you see on the surface of the lake.

disposal system. This consists of a septic tank and drain field. If the system is functioning properly, it will remove most health-threatening organisms and some chemical substances from your wastewater before it reaches surface or groundwater systems. Water-soluble substances are not removed, however, so the location and proper functioning of your septic system is important to you and the lake. Even properly designed septic systems eventually need to be replaced. Consider whether a replacement site is available before buying or building.

Of Course You Need a Permit. If you do need to build or replace your system, locate a state-certified contractor to do the work. Either the contractor or you will need to contact your County Sanitarian for regulations and to acquire a permit. Counties have ordinances concerning septic system placement. They can't be placed in floodplains and wetlands and must be specific distances away from wells, lakes, and streams. Several factors, including slope, water table depth, and soil type will be used to decide which septic system type can be used.

You can get information on septic tank requirements, health regulations and permitting procedures from your county health department, soil conservation service office, and county Extension office. Information on septic system maintenance and operation can be obtained from the Florida Cooperative Extension Service and also from the Florida Septic Tank Association (see "For More Information" at the end of this chapter).

Types of Systems. The most common septic system has a tank buried in the ground near the house. It may be steel, concrete, or fiberglass. If you have a septic system with a buried opening and you don't know where it is, you can use a rod to probe for the location. An area where the ground appears to have settled may indicate its whereabouts.

You can get information on septic tank requirements, health regulations and permitting procedures from your county health department, soil conservation service office, and county Extension office.

The following diagram shows the generalized structure of a septic system. Within the tank, heavy materials settle out, baffles keep floating materials from leaving and the liquid flows out into a drain field by gravity (or perhaps by a pump). As the liquid flows through, these waste substances are broken down or filtered out. Plants above the drain field will take up some water and the rest will either go to the surface and evaporate or eventually reach the groundwater. It has been shown recently that a two-foot layer of fine sand under the drainfield is about as effective in removing pollutants as a sewage treatment plant.

Under some conditions a mound system may be necessary. In situations where a buried drain field is unsuitable (because of soil type, bedrock, water table depth, etc.), the drain field is elevated rather than buried and the liquid wastes are pumped up to it. An elevated drain field generally is more costly than a buried one.

Sometimes conditions do not allow the replacement of a failed septic system and a holding tank must be used. This is a water-tight tank which is pumped regularly to a truck which delivers the contents to a waste-water treatment plant or approved area for spreading on land. This can be expensive if pumping has to be done frequently but may be no problem for a cottage or home which is not used continuously.

If the System Fails... How will you know if the system fails? At the extreme, you may smell runoff or your system may back up in

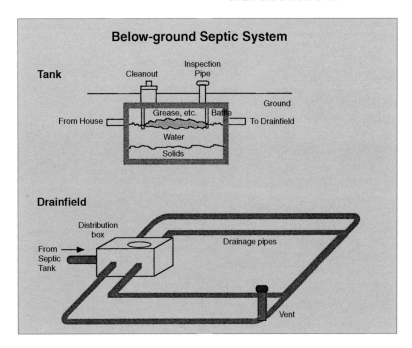

Below-ground Septic System

the house. If you are buying, ask when the tank was last pumped. Remove the access cover and check to see if the baffles are in place and how high the liquid level is. A very high liquid level may indicate that clogging is preventing water from getting to the drain field. If the liquid level is very low, there may be a hole in the tank. If your drain field is clogged, it will need to be replaced.

Other symptoms which may warn you of trouble in your septic system are plumbing backups or slow flushing in the toilet, plumbing noises, mushy areas in the yard, very green areas in the yard, or low spots beginning to appear in the yard.

Keeping Your Septic System Healthy. Several things are recommended to keep your system function correctly. Keep surface water from flowing into your drain field. Don't drive or park on it or allow trees or shrubs to put roots into it and clog the pipes. Regularly pump your tank. Keep use of a garbage disposal to a minimum. Avoid materials such as grease, which may clog the drains, and chemicals, which may kill the organisms which break down the wastes.

A poorly functioning system can be a health hazard if it contaminates wells or ground water. Such a system can also allow pollutants as well as nutrients to reach the lake, reducing water quality and producing changes in the plants and animals living there.

…a Drop to Drink

Unless your lakefront property is within a municipality, you will need a well — one that can provide safe drinking water. Most drinking water comes from groundwater from aquifers. If the well is already present, don't assume the water is safe without having it tested. Waterfront properties often have wells which are shallow and more likely to be contaminated since

A poorly functioning septic system can be a health hazard if it contaminates wells or ground water.

ground-water may be close to the surface near lakes. It is likely that you will not be able to get financing without a wellwater safety test.

Property With Existing Wells. If you are buying a house which has a well, check to see if meets codes, its depth, age, type of water pump, and pressure tank. Check the rate of flow (8–10 gal/minute is acceptable for a well less than 100 feet in depth). Check the location of the well relative to the septic system (it should be at least 75 feet away) and other possible contamination sources. The most common types of contamination are bacterial, some types of metals, chlorides, nitrates, and organics.

Testing Your Wellwater. It is probably a good idea to have your water tested if land use has changed near you, if you made plumbing repairs, if there is a change in taste, odor, or appearance, if a neighbor's well is found to be unsafe, or if you begin to use a well which has not been recently used.

Tests include coliform bacteria, nitrates, lead, and oil products (if a landfill is nearby). County health departments or university Extension agents can suggest certified labs that do these tests and schedules for testing. Florida law (F.A.C.62-22) has testing requirements which vary according to the number of people the well or water supply is serving. If your water comes from a community water supply which serves more than 15 year-round residents, it must be periodically tested. Those serving more than 1000 are regularly tested for a number of kinds of contamination.

In addition to being a requirement when a well is installed, bacterial testing should be done routinely (this is required by many county health departments). The major indicator of drinking water sanitary quality is the bacterial coliform count (Maximum Contaminant Level (MCL) = average 1 per 100 ml water).

It is probably a good idea to have your water tested if land use has changed near you.

Your local health department can run bacterial tests and, if needed, other tests. If you simply want to know what chemicals are in your water, a private lab can test it. You will need to get a reliable sample which is representative of your water supply. (For sampling methods, see "Home Water Quality and Safety" listed under "For More Information" at the end of this chapter.)

Nitrates. If land use in your area suggests that agricultural fertilizers or organic waste disposal might allow nitrates to enter your well, you should have the water tested. High nitrate levels are a particular concern for infants. Nitrates are converted in the body to nitrites, which alter the blood's ability to carry oxygen. Nitrate levels should be no higher than 10 mg/L as nitrogen. Some banks require nitrate testing before a mortgage will be approved.

If You Need a New Well. If you build on an undeveloped site, and will not be connecting to a public water supply, you probably will need a private well drilled. Florida DEP has the given responsibility for regulating water wells to the water management districts; therefore, the WMD should always be contacted before doing anything involving wells. This will ensure that needed permits will be obtained, and statutes and rules followed. It may prevent well drilling in contaminated areas. Your first step is to find a licensed contractor to drill the well. You must have a licensed contractor to construct your well (unless you are putting in a well less than 2 inches in diameter, for example, a shallow well for irrigation).

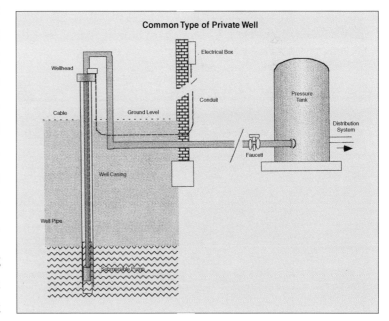

Getting Your Well Drilled. If you are building a house, your building contractor will arrange with a well driller to construct your well. The driller must obtain permits and conform with local and state regulations. Generally, wells should be drilled on ground high enough to prevent runoff contamination and at least 75 feet from septic tanks and drainage fields. There are minimum distances above ground level for wellheads and depth of wells relative to groundwater. Consider a deep well if there is risk of local contamination.

If there is an abandoned well on your property, or you wish to abandon an existing well, contact your water management district or regional DEP office for instructions on proper abandonment procedures. If your well is in need of repair, hire a licensed contractor and be sure your water management district is contacted for a permit.

You will need a pressure tank as part of your home water supply system to control the flow from your well. This will regulate water flow so you can draw a small amount such as a glass of water. Water in the pressure tank will supply small uses and your pump will run only when the pressure in the tank drops to a preset level. Your contractor or well driller will recommend tank size and include it as a part of the system.

Docks and Stuff

If you live on the waterfront, chances are that you will have a boat and need a place to moor it and a structure from which you can load and unload the boat. You may also want to swim from a dock extending out into the water. In some areas of the country, it was once fashionable to construct boathouses out over the water, housing boats and occasionally guests of the owner. This kind of construction is now regulated and often prohibited and **any kind of construction adjacent to or on the water is regulated by both state and local ordinances.**

A dock (pier) awaits a boater on Lake Conway.

Mark Brenner

A "dock" for swimming, fishing, tying up your boat or simply relaxing, may be perpendicular to the shoreline (pier) or parallel to and against the shore (wharf). You might build a wharf if the water near the shore is deep enough; more often the nearshore area is shallow and a pier allows you to extend to deeper water which will clear your boat's draft. Docks can be built by the waterfront property owner in the "riparian zone". This is the area included if your property lines are extended into the water perpendicular to the shoreline.

You do not need a permit from the Department of Environmental Protection or your water management district[1] to construct a noncommercial private dock of less than 1000 square feet over the water. (Less than 500 if it is located in "Outstanding Florida Waters"). It must be the sole dock for at least 65 feet (unless the property platted has less than 65 feet of shoreline, in which case there may be one per lot). You can also construct boat lifts, boat shelters or gazebos above the dock area; however, they cannot be enclosed with walls or doors, be lived in, or exceed the size limit above. Boat shelters have roofs and may house boat lifts. They provide shelter for a single watercraft and are regulated in size. A boathouse has walls as well as a roof. They cannot be built over the water.

Be sure to check with your local municipality, county, or lake association to see if they have additional regulations or "pier zones" which determine the maximum length of a pier into the water.

Docks cannot interfere with public rights or navigation. The regulations cited above define the size of a dock. They generally are built only as wide as necessary for safety; six feet is common. Your dock can be floating or on

Be sure to check with your local municipality, county or lake association to see if they have additional regulations or "pier zones" which determine the maximum length of a pier into the water.

[1] No permit shall be required under chapters 40B-4 or 40B-400, Florida Administrative Code.

pilings or posts and cannot involve filling or dredging other than needed to install the post. If water levels vary, floating ones may be more practical.

Decks cannot be built over the water; like houses and other structures, decks must be set back from the water (usually 75 feet).

Swimming rafts (diving platforms) are common on northern lakes, but are not used very much in Florida. They probably make very handy alligator basking sites, so perhaps you might be better off without one. If you do want one, you should check your local and county administration first to see if they are allowed on your lake. If they are, call your DEP regional office (see Chapter 7 map) to determine whether a state permit is needed.

When There's a Dam on Your Site

Should you buy a piece of property with a dam on it? Dams can be hazardous, either because of the safety hazards of using water near an intact dam or because of the human and property risks associated with failure of the dam. Also, if you buy property which includes a dam, you must have the financial ability to maintain it. Carefully check out the legal aspects of buying property which contains a dam, even if you plan to remove it.

Removing, altering, or building a dam requires a permit from the DEP. You also need to contact your water management district, especially if it is located on a navigable stream. It might also be necessary to contact the Army Corps of Engineers. Maps and phone numbers of regional offices for all three agencies are listed in Chapter 13. This applies both to concrete or metal structures and those made of earth.

The Department of Environmetnal Protection and the water management districts have agreements concerning permitting where the interests of both

Carefully check out the legal aspects of buying property which contains a dam, even if you plan to remove it.

are involved. These agreements are intended to make the permitting process more efficient. The process differs, however, depending upon which water management district has jurisdiction in your area. In general, DEP handles "systems" at the individual homeowner level and should be the permitting agency.

Landscaping Your Lakefront Property

*...a lush green lawn sweeps to the lake
along with flowers for wildlife's sake.*

Whether you build on undeveloped property or buy a lakefront home, landscaping decisions you make should reflect both your individual tastes and your concern for the lake on which you will be living. After all, your decision to live on a lake or river probably included a search for something on a "good" lake. Whatever the criteria you used, you have a vested interest in helping to keep your lake as beautiful and useful as possible.

Lawns vs. Natural Areas. Should you as a lakefront homeowner retain the natural vegetation between the house and the lake or remove it to grow a lawn? This decision will depend upon your own personal tastes and what gives you enjoyment. Some people want their property as natural as possible, to increase their enjoyment of native vegetation and wildlife. Others like to see the sweeping green lawn in their view of the lake. If a lawn is your choice, there are things you can do to minimize its effects on the lake.

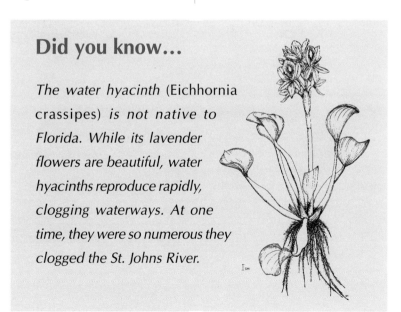

Did you know...

The water hyacinth (Eichhornia crassipes) is not native to Florida. While its lavender flowers are beautiful, water hyacinths reproduce rapidly, clogging waterways. At one time, they were so numerous they clogged the St. Johns River.

Fertilize Your Lawn, Not the Lake. Those who have lawns from the house down to the lake like to see a nice sweep of green. The applications of fertilizer used to achieve this may also reach the lake, adding nutrients to the water. These nutrients, particularly nitrogen and phosphorus, are absorbed by algae and aquatic plants, making the lake more productive, creating greener water and denser aquatic plant growth. What can we do to have our lawns and protect our lake at the same time?

You can save money and time and help your lake by reducing the amount and frequency of fertilization. Use fertilizers only when necessary. Minimize the use of fertilizers which contain phosphorus. Using a complete fertilizer in March and September has been suggested as a minimum program. This can result in less mowing, less thatch buildup, less need for irrigation, and fewer insect and disease problems. (See "Florida Lawn Handbook" and other publications listed under "For More Information" at the end of this chapter.)

Consider using liquid foliage fertilizers which can be taken up immediately by the grass after application. Solid fertilizers can be applied during dry spells and immediately irrigated to move the particles into the soil. (Slow-release types may be easily dissolved by rainfall, and either the released nutrients or the particles themselves may reach the lake.) Use of swales and berms as well as buffer strips of natural vegetation between the lawn and the lake can help control runoff of fertilizers.

For some of our lakes, phosphorus is a key nutrient in the productivity of the lake. Increased phosphorus can result in green water due to algal blooms or denser aquatic plant growth. Be sure to use detergents containing low amounts of phosphorus (less than 0.5%). Whether used outside for washing cars or inside where it goes into your septic system, the phosphorus from detergents can reach the lake.

You can save money and time and help your lake by reducing the amount and frequency of fertilization.

Other Lawn Tips. Mow your lawn often enough so no more than one third of the grass leaf is cut with a sharp blade. Leave clippings on the lawn to provide nutrients as they decompose, reducing the need for fertilizers.

Consider landscaping your property in terms of protecting your lake and at the same time reducing work for yourself — leaving you more time to enjoy lake living! Low-maintenance landscaping involves reduced fertilization, simple design, mulching, alternate ground covers to grass, and use of native and low-maintenance plants. Rather than over-fertilize, learn to identify plants with nutrient deficiencies, thus fertilizing only when needed. You can thus reduce the use of pesticides, herbicides and fertilizer, institute practices which keep what is used out of the lake, and save money and time.

Attracting Birds and Butterflies. When planning your landscaping, for example if you have a buffer strip, keep the birds and butterflies in mind. Including some of their favorite plants can provide you with a great deal of enjoyment.

When planning your landscaping, for example if you have a buffer strip, keep the birds and butterflies in mind.

Plants with colorful and attractive fruit provide food for birds and you with an opportunity to observe them. Other plants provide nesting and/or perching spots. Some, such as trumpet vine, have flowers which provide nectar for hummingbirds.

There are many sources of information to guide you in choices (see "For More Information" at the end of this chapter). There are also some useful publications devoted to the attraction of butterflies. Current interest in butterflies is shown by the number of "butterfly gardens" open to the public in Florida and other states. This has resulted in a variety of new literature to help those who want more in their gardens. Most of us enjoy seeing their beautiful colors flitting in and out of our plants.

Butterflies use some flowers as nectar; other plants provide food for the caterpillars during the butterfly larval stage. Pentas and butterfly weed are good choices.

Preventing Stormwater Runoff. We are all familiar with Florida rainstorms, which can dump several inches of water in a short time. Under natural conditions, stormwater runs down the slope to the lake, and passes through natural vegetation which slows its flow. This allows debris and particulate materials to settle out while water and its dissolved substances soak in.

Here in Florida, slopes are usually gentle because our changes in elevation from shore to lake are small. However, lakefront homes are likely to be built up on pads of substrate, keeping the house dry and allowing for a lawn. Native vegetation is likely to be removed between the house and the shoreline. Stormwater moves quickly off rooftops and paved areas.

Running over drives and patios, stormwater picks up oil and debris. As it moves across the lawn, it adds herbicides, fertilizers, and pesticides, which were applied to the lawn, and runs into the lake. Instead of being absorbed into the soil as it proceeds down the gradient, stormwater runoff not only brings unwanted materials into the lake but may erode shoreline as it flows.

Landscaping and site development plans should take into account where stormwater will go and include means to slow down its movement. Constructing a swale and berm system and/or a buffer strip can help you slow the runoff of rainwater, preventing some of these problems.

Creating Berms and Swales. A swale is a low area followed by a higher one called a berm. Rainwater runoff will slow as it moves from the low swale to higher berm, causing less erosion and allowing nutrients to be absorbed and

Landscaping and site development plans should take into account where stormwater will go and include means to slow down its movement.

particles to settle out in the vegetation. Allowing natural vegetation to fill in the swale will increase this absorption/settling out process and help to prevent erosion and the nutrient enrichment of the lake.

Buffer Strips. Buffer strips of natural vegetation between the lawn or landscaped area and the lake can help reduce water runoff to the lake. For the sandy areas with gentle slopes that are common in Florida, a 25-foot-wide buffer strip of natural vegetation can be very effective in preventing nutrients and contaminants from reaching the lake. On steeper slopes, buffer strips must be wider.

A sinkhole retention pond adds beauty to the J. Wayne Reitz Student Union on the UF campus.

If you have a lawn down to the water, leave an unmowed strip along the shore. If you also leave a strip extending inland along a natural contour, native flowers and other plants will grow, creating interest and trapping nutrients and other materials during runoff. You may also want to plant native trees and shrubs, which can now be obtained from many nurseries.

Stormwater Retention Ponds. Some of you may live on waterbodies which were constructed as stormwater retention ponds (or are connected to such waterbodies). Created by developers as a response to legislation designed to reduce the pollution capabilities of stormwater runoff, management of these ponds rests with the homeowners' associations. Permits for such systems are obtained from your water management district. Check both local and state regulations before adding or removing aquatic plants.

Since these retention ponds are created to receive runoff from storm events, they accumulate nutrients, pollutants, and sediments. Some are relatively shallow, permitting aquatic plants to grow. (Sometimes the sides are bulkheaded, producing straight sides where plants cannot grow.) Such nutrient-enriched ponds may also develop algal blooms.

How much you can do ecologically in maintaining ponds depends upon many things — pond depth and presence or absence of bulkheading among others. You may decide to plant native or other shoreline or littoral plants, for aesthetics or to control algae. Degree of success in algal or macrophyte control and fish survival will probably not be the same as in a natural lake.

Shoreline vegetation. Shoreline vegetation helps control erosion and provides homes for wildlife whose habitat is the lake's edge. It provides nesting sites for birds, hiding and foraging sites for frogs, turtles, and others.

Removal of shoreline vegetation to form a sandy beach or lawn removes wildlife habitat and allows stormwater to run off rapidly. Clearing only part of your shoreline allows a small sandy beach and/or open access to the water and retains most of the beneficial effects of the natural shoreline vegetation.

Landscape Your Shoreline? Landscaping at the water's edge and the littoral zone is called **aquascaping**. You might want to aquascape if you are renovating a lakeshore from which the natural vegetation was previously removed, developing the shoreline areas of a retention pond, or wish to replace noxious exotics with desirable plants. To do this, you need to be familiar with the value and kinds of aquatic plants and what is legal.

For More Information...

Selecting Your Waterfront Home

Florida Lakes: A Description of Lakes, Their Processes and Means of Protection.
    by H. Lee Edmiston and V.B. Myers. 1983. Water Quality Management and Restoration, Department of Environmental Regulation. Tallahassee, Fla. Wilderness Graphics, Inc. Tallahassee, Fla.
Management Guide for Lakes and Rivers.
    North American Lake Management Society. Madison, Wis.

Thomas Wright

Shoreline vegetation can be considered aquascaping.

Building Your Waterfront Home

Air Conditioning, Moisture, and Mildew.
> Institute of Food and Agricultural Sciences, University of Florida. Gainesville, Fla. Florida Cooperative Extension Service Fact Sheet EES-302.

Closing your Florida home.
> Institute of Food and Agricultural Science, University of Florida, Gainesville, Fla. Florida Cooperative Extension Service videotape SV-333. 16 min.

How to Close Your Florida Home.
> by Virginia Peart. Institute of Food and Agricultural Sciences, University of Florida. Gainesville, Fla. Florida Cooperative Extension Service Fact Sheet EES-66.

Say Goodbye to Mildew and Save Energy.
> by Virginia Peart. Institute of Food and Agricultural Sciences, University of Florida. Gainesville, Fla. Florida Cooperative Extension Service Fact Sheet EES-64.

Design Considerations for Wooden Structures in Florida.
> by G.E. Sherwood. Institute of Food and Agricultural Sciences, University of Florida. Gainesville, Fla. Florida Cooperative Extension Service Circular 538.

Septic System

Florida Septic Tank Association
> PO Box 1025
> Lakeland, FL 33802

Home Septic Systems: Proper Care and Maintenance.
> by Ken M. Lomax. Delaware Cooperative Extension Service, Univ. of Delaware. Newark, Del.

A Homeowner's Guide to Septic Systems.
> by Torsten D. Sponenberg, Jacob H. Kahn, and Kathryn P. Sevebeck. 1985. Virginia Polytechnic Institute and State University, Virginia. Water Resources Research Center. Blacksburg, Va.

Keep It Clean: A Citizen's Guide to Protecting Our Estuary.
> by Carla Kappmeyer. 1993. Rookery Bay National Estuaries Research Reserves, Florida Division of Natural Resources; National Oceanic and Atmospheric Administration, Sanctuaries and Reserves Division; and South Florida WMD.

Your Home Septic System.
> by R.B. Brown and M.V. Peart. 1993. Institute for Food and Agricultural Sciences, University of Florida. Gainesville, Fla. Florida Cooperative Extension Service Fact Sheet SL-59.

Water Wells

Handbook of Florida Water Regulation.
> by M.T. Olexa. 1991. Institute of Food and Agricultural Sciences, University of Florida. Gainesville, Fla. Florida Cooperative Extension Service Circular 1026.

Permits required for building on a lake can be extensive.

Home Water Quality and Safety.
>D.Z. Haman and D.B. Bottcher. 1986. Institute of Food and Agricultural Sciences, University of Florida. Gainesville, Fla. Florida Cooperative Extension Service Circular 703.

Selection of Pressure Tanks for Water Supply Systems.
>by A.G. Smajstria, F.S. Zazueta, and D.Z. Haman. 1986. Institute of Food and Agricultural Sciences, University of Florida. Gainesville, Fla. Florida Cooperative Extension Service Circular 741.

Water Wells for Florida Irrigation Systems.
>by D.Z. Haman, A.G. Smajstrla, and G.A. Clark. 1993. Institute of Food and Agricultural Sciences, University of Florida. Gainesville, Fla. Florida Cooperative Extension Service Circular 803.

Landscaping Your Property

You can obtain further information on specific aquatic plants, their biology and control by contacting:
>Aquatic Plant Information Retrieval System
>Center for Aquatic Plants, University of Florida
>7922 NW 71st St.
>Gainesville, FL 32653

Butterfly Gardening with Florida's Native Plants.
>by C. Huegel. Florida Native Plant Society.

A Citizen's Guide to Stormwater Ponds.
>Southwest Florida Water Management District. Brooksville, Fla.

Establishing Your Florida Lawn.
>by L.B. McCarty. 1994. Institute of Food and Agricultural Sciences, University of Florida. Gainesville, Fla. Florida Cooperative Extension Service Fact Sheet ENH-03.

Fertilizer Management: Key to a Sound Water Quality Program.
>by D. Bottcher and D. Rhue. 1984. Institute of Food and Agricultural Sciences, University of Florida. Gainesville, Fla. Florida Cooperative Extension Service publication SP-28.

Florida Lawn Handbook.
>by Kathleen C. Ruppert and Robert J. Black. 1995. Institute of Food and Agricultural Sciences, University of Florida. Gainesville, Fla. Florida Cooperative Extension Service publication SP-45. 224 pp.

Florida Yards and Neighborhoods Handbook.
>1994. Institute of Food and Agricultural Sciences, University of Florida. Gainesville, Fla. Florida Cooperative Extension Service Bulletin 295. 56 pp.

General Recommendations for Fertilization of Turfgrasses on Florida Soils.
>by J.B. Sartain. 1990. Institute of Food and Agricultural Sciences, University of Florida. Gainesville, Fla. Florida Cooperative Extension Service Fact Sheet SL-21.

Thomas Wright

Landscaping your lakeside property can prevent erosion and provide habitat for wildlife.

Homeowner's Guide to Stormwater Runoff.
St. Johns River Water Management District. Palatka, Fla.

An Introduction to Aquascaping.
by Frank Mazotti. 1990. Institute of Food and Agricultural Sciences, University of Florida. Gainesville, Fla. Florida Cooperative Extension Service Fact Sheet SS-WIS-04.

Landscaping for Wildlife.
by C.L. Henderson. *LakeLine*, Vol. 16, No. 1, pp. 14–15, 44. North American Lake Management Society.

Low Maintenance Landscapes.
by D.F. Hamilton and R.J. Black. Institute of Food and Agricultural Sciences, University of Florida. Gainesville, Fla. Florida Cooperative Extension Service Fact Sheet OH-24.

Native Florida Plants for Home Landscapes.
by D.F. Hamilton and R.J. Black. Institute of Food and Agricultural Sciences, University of Florida. Gainesville, Fla. Florida Cooperative Extension Service Fact Sheet ENH-25.

Native Plants that Attract Wildlife: Central Florida.
by C. Huegel. Institute of Food and Agricultural Sciences, University of Florida. Gainesville, Fla. Florida Cooperative Extension Service Fact Sheet SS-WIS-09.

Preparing to Plant a Florida Lawn.
by L.B. McCarty. 1994. Institute of Food and Agricultural Sciences, University of Florida. Gainesville, Fla. Florida Cooperative Extension Service Fact Sheet ENH-02.

Plant Nutrient Deficiency Symptoms.
by J.J. Street and N. Gammon. Institute of Food and Agricultural Sciences, University of Florida. Gainesville, Fla. Florida Cooperative Extension Service Circular 435.

Stormwater Management: A Guide for Floridians.
by E.H. Livingston and E. McCarron. Florida Department of Environmental Regulation. Tallahassee, Fla. 72 pp.

Your Florida Landscape: A Complete Guide to Planting and Maintenance.
by Robert J. Black and Kathleen C. Ruppert. 1997. Institute of Food and Agricultural Sciences, University of Florida. Gainesville, Fla. Florida Cooperative Extension Service publication SP-135. 234 pp. ❦

Lake vegetation frames a view of Santa Fe Lake.

CHAPTER 6

Protecting Your Lake

…Plan ahead and work together, help your lake to stay in shape.

Usually, people live at the lake because they like what lakefront living provides; the pleasure of looking at the water and/or the recreational benefits the lake provides. So most of them feel that they have a vested interest in seeing that the lake stays healthy and suitable for these purposes.

Throughout this book, we have provided suggestions and alternatives relative to lakefront living which can help you or your efforts to improve the lake. Most of these are things the individual lakefront owner or lake user can do: suggestions for reducing runoff into the lake through house and septic construction, landscaping, practicing safety in boating, swimming and water-skiing.

Individuals also can collect litter, be considerate neighbors, be aware of proposed legislation, and support legislation and candidates promoting good water resource protection. However, working with others to improve or maintain your lake's quality can achieve results an individual cannot.

Lake Associations

A lake association is a group of people working together to solve common problems relative to their particular lake. It may be very informal or more formal if needed. Generally, informal associations focus more on social and educational goals. Formal ones may incorporate so they can apply for grants and raise money to solve problems. Serious lake problems involve everyone living on or using the lake; the lake association provides a forum for reaching solutions.

You may wish to join or start a lake association. If you already have one, be active in achieving its goals. If not, you can get together with others and form one. A lake association can have many benefits, not the least of which is the sense of community you get by becoming acquainted with and developing partnerships with your neighbors. You may want to have a newsletter to keep everyone abreast of news on or about the lake. You could organize fund-raising events to raise money or apply for a grant to help your lake.

If your lake is being monitored (for example, through Florida LAKEWATCH; see below) or already receiving help through state efforts (such as lakes which are part of the SWIM program), you can keep in touch as a group and perhaps be volunteer monitors.

Your homeowners association might have educational programs for your members and the surrounding community. The North American Lake Management Society (NALMS) has videos on a variety of lake-related topics which you can rent. The University of Florida's Institute for Food and Agricultural Sciences (UF/IFAS) has videos on lake quality and aquatic plant control which can be purchased. (See "For More Information" at the end of this chapter.) The group can act collectively in expressing opinions and needs to local government officials or state agencies.

A lake association can have many benefits, not the least of which is the sense of community you get by becoming acquainted with and developing partnerships with your neighbors.

Looking at a Lake Through Time

Like all natural things, lakes change over time — from season to season and from year to year. This makes lakes interesting but also means that it is difficult to sort out what is causing the changes. Long-term data are needed to distinguish natural cycles from changes which are permanently degrading lake water quality. One lake for which such data is available is Lake Alto.

Lake Alto is a 540-acre lake located in Alachua County, Florida near the city of Waldo. Newcomers to the lake are often amazed at the changes they see in and around the lake throughout the year. This is true of most Florida lakes. Seasonal changes are evident in a large number of lakes sampled by Florida LAKEWATCH. For example, some years had low rainfall and drought conditions; in other years (1997–98), heavy rainfall led to increased lake levels, and some areas were flooded. These changes are part of the natural cycles we see in lakes. These changes are confirmed by samples collected throughout the year at many lakes, and in cases like Lake Alto, these samples have been taken for many years.

Natural cycles can be seen in the water chemistry data provided by Florida LAKEWATCH. An example of the chlorophyll data is included here. Most Florida lakes experience their highest chlorophyll concentrations during late summer and early fall. Generally, changes throughout the year are no more that 30% higher or lower than the annual average for most lakes. However, individual lakes may experience greater changes, which at first seem striking but are well within the natural cyles or expected range of variability when studied over several years.

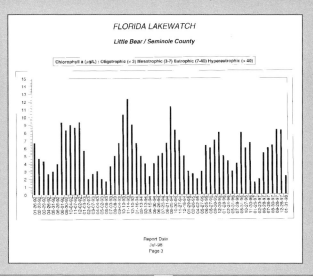

Lake associations can provide the opportunity for a group of lakefront property owners to get together at intervals and keep communication open. Or, associations can be highly organized and active, effective in helping to improve the quality of their lake, its ecosystem and surrounding watershed. If there isn't one on your lake, consider organizing one yourself.

The SWIM Program

In 1987, Florida passed the Surface Water Improvement and Management Act (SWIM) to improve and restore polluted waters — lakes, rivers, bays, estuaries. SWIM was implemented on a regional basis by the Water Management Districts. A priority list of waters most in need of help was drawn up in each region. Management plans are being developed first for those with highest priority. (For examples, see "A Guide to Protecting Our Surface Waters" listed in "For More Information" at the end of this chapter.)

Florida LAKEWATCH

LAKEWATCH is a volunteer lake monitoring program administered through the Department of Fisheries and Aquatic Sciences at the University of Florida. More than 400 lakes are part of the program which involves citizen monitors who sample and measure water quality parameters on a regular basis. Samples are sent to Gainesville for analysis, and results sent back to the volunteers. If you would like to be a part of LAKEWATCH, contact the Director; however, present resources won't cover all requests, so be prepared to be on a waiting list.

"It's All Politics" — Politics and Politicians

How often we all hear, "Oh, it's all politics, there is nothing we can do about it". Well, often you can. In fact, most of us think about our politicians,

Doug Colle

A LAKEWATCH volunteer collects water samples.

local and state, only when we want to complain. Why not work with them when there are problems to be solved or things to be done? Most of them would welcome information and help. You as an individual and your lake association can often make a very real difference if you get involved in a positive way. Your elected officials can do a better job if they are better informed and know they are working with your support.

"Closing the Door"

Living on a lake brings both benefits and problems. Problems arise because many people want to enjoy a diverse and often incompatible set of activities. As populations increase, lake use and recreation conflicts will also increase. You may feel your lake and your quality of life are being threatened.

You might wish to "close the door" to more people, to public access, or to activities which you see as harmful. While "closing the door" usually is impractical, you will still want to protect your lake. No-wake zones and/or separating activities by time or space may be solutions. This is when a lake association with regular communication and a history of working together can turn conflict into cooperation.

Joining Societies

You or your lake association may wish to be a member of the North American Lake Management Society (NALMS) and/or the Florida Lake Management Society (the state chapter of NALMS). Newsletters, *LakeLine*, and annual

Did you know...

Did you know that Florida is famous for its disappearing lakes? For example, Iamonia Lake, Lake Jackson, Lafayette Lake, and Micosukee Lake, all in Leon County; Alligator Lake (Columbia County) and Alachua Lake (now Paynes Prairie in Alachua County) have all either lost much of or all of their water when sinkholes opened up. Sinkholes may fill in or water tables may rise and water levels may be regained.

meetings give citizens and management professionals the chance to interact and learn from each other. Interacting with members of other lake associations and learning about problems and solutions can benefit your own lake association.

Plan Ahead!

One of the most important things you can do for your lake is to develop a management plan.

One of the most important things you can do for your lake is to develop a management plan. Unless you already have a developed plan, for example through the SWIM program, work through your lake association, enlist the aid of personnel from appropriate management agencies and local government. Planning ahead cooperatively with everyone involved can make change easier to adjust to, protect your lake from pollution, reduce nutrient inflow, and reduce conflicts.

For More Information…

The North American Lake Management Society (NALMS) offers numerous videos that can be rented by either members or non-members. You can contact NALMS for titles and prices:

> North American Lake Management Society
> PO Box 5443
> Madison, Wis. 53707
> Tel. (608) 233-3186 or Fax (608) 233-3186

Aquatics. Quarterly publication of the Florida Aquatic Plant Management Society.
> Ken Langeland, editor. Center for Aquatic Plants. Gainesville, Fla.

A Citizen's Guide to Lake Protection.
> Freshwater Foundation and Minnesota Pollution Control Agency. 1985. Freshwater Foundation, 725 County Road Six, Wazata, Minn. 55391 or call (612) 449-0092. 16 pp.

Citizen Monitoring.
> *LakeLine*, Sept. 1993. North American Lake Management Society. Madison, Wis.

A Guide to Protecting Our Surface Waters.
> Northwest Florida Water Management District Office of Public Information, Route 1, Box 3100, Havana, Fla. 32333.

Handling Conflicts on Your Lake.
> by Karen Vigmostad. 1996. Ecovision Associates, 76 E. Sherwood Rd., Williamson, Mo. 48895-9435.

Lake and Reservoir Restoration Guidance Manual.
> 1990. North American Lake Management Society. Madison, Wis. 326 pp.

The Lake Book: Actions You Can Take to Protect Your Lake.
> 1993. Congress of Lake Associations, RR 2, Box 391, Bayview St., Yarmouth, Maine 04096. You can also call (207) 846-4271 for price and information on how to customize this publication for your lake.

Lake Conservation Handbook.
> 1990. North American Lake Management Society. Madison, Wis. 20 pp.

LakeLine.
> North American Lake Management Society. Madison, Wis. Quarterly.

Monitoring Lake and Reservoir Restoration.
> 1990. North American Lake Management Society. Madison, Wis. 566 pp.

Resources Catalog.
> 1998. Institute of Food and Agricultural Sciences, University of Florida. Gainesville, Fla. Florida Cooperative Extension Service publication SP-1. This catalog includes videos as well as publications related to lakes and aquatic plant control.

Starting and Building an Effective Lake Association.
> North American Lake Management Society. Madison, Wis.

Understanding Lake Data.
> by Byron Shaw, Christine Mechenich, and Lowell Klessig. Wisconsin Extension Service, University of Wisconsin. Madison, Wis. Wisconsin Extension publication G-3582. You can order this publication by mail from Extension Publications, Rm 245, 30 N. Murray St., Madison, Wis. or call (608) 262-3346. ❧

Did you know...

Did you know that fishermen can sometimes "smell the fish" in a lake? Spawning aggregations of fish can leave oil on the surface, producing a "slick-like" appearance. People can smell this and go fishing in that spot!

CHAPTER 7

Agencies, Laws, and Regulations

*…if you want to construct or change anything
on your lakefront property, make sure it is legal.*

Whether you are a present or prospective lakefront property owner, sooner or later you will want to make some alteration to your property or to the lakeshore. Chances are that change requires a permit or may fall under some local, state, or federal regulation. You need to be aware of your rights and responsibilities as owners of property on the water, which state and federal agencies are concerned with water regulations, the major laws and programs related to water and how local governmental actions may affect you. In this section we provide you with an introduction to this complex area of living on the lake and information which may help in locating the right agency when you need one.

Authors' Note…Be informed and be legal

Florida has many agencies concerned with environmental resource regulation. The state laws are complex and not easy for the average person to understand. Also, laws change. You may get different answers from inquiries to agency personnel because regulations are so complex, and there are so many exemptions and exceptions. We have tried to give you our best summary of the regulations as they are applied based on the Florida Statutes and the Florida Administrative Code. However, we cannot include all of the exceptions, and if we did, someone else might interpret them differently. And, by the time you read this, some of these regulations and laws will have changed! **To be on safe legal ground, before you do anything which affects the lakefront, wildlife, plants, or the lake, get informed, then contact the appropriate agency(s).** You can get a copy of the Wildlife Code through your regional office of the Florida Game and Fresh Water Fish Commission. Copies of the Florida Statutes and the Florida Administrative Code are in libraries and in the offices of your state representatives.

Rights and Responsibilities of Living on the Lakefront

As a lakefront property owner, you may have privileges that other folks don't, but you also have certain responsibilities. Many lakes and rivers are public land and open to public use. So state and local governments, and in some cases the federal government, have statutes, ordinances, and regulations which affect how you use the lake on which you live, the lake itself, and how you relate to other users.

Water has always been important to people. As a source of drinking water, as a highway, and as a place for recreation. Because of this basic importance of water and attractiveness of water bodies, there are nearly always competing and often incompatible interests for its use.

Here in Florida, we have over 7000 lakes, many rivers, springs, swamps, bays, and estuaries. Shouldn't that be enough water so that we wouldn't need regulations? We also have a large population which either impacts these

As a lakefront property owner, you may have privileges that other folks don't, but you also have certain responsibilities.

waters through the water needs and waste products of cities or impacts waterbodies directly through personal use. We want to use and live on our lakes and rivers; we also want them clean, attractive, and safe. We want to fish, go boating and swim, but we also need to do this safely. Thus at various levels, governmental units regulate our waters and our water supply.

Public vs. Private. As a lakefront property owner, you own to the shoreline and have exclusive use of that area ("riparian rights"). Except for some private, non-navigable lakes without public access, you do not own the lake bottom. The state owns the lake bottom, the water and any fish and wildlife in it. Regulations protect both the lake and the shoreline.

Different agencies have different responsibilities for protecting the waterbody and regulating use. For example, if you want to install a dock, the lake bottom (substrate) in which you sink your posts is the responsibility of the Florida Department of Environmental Protection (DEP). However, the effect of the dock, on water flow or boat traffic, for instance, also would be of interest to your water management district, thus you might need a permit from both agencies.

Fortunately, the DEP and the water management districts have operating agreements intended to make the permitting process more efficient. (A call to DEP or to your water management district would enable you to get the necessary information for permit applications.) Some local governments will require a permit.

Did you know...

Did you know that the most important group of sinkhole lakes in the New World occurs in the state of Florida? Why so many sinkholes in Florida? Much of Florida is underlain by limestone rocks. Over long periods of time, as water seeps downward through cracks in the rock, the water slowly dissolves the limestone to form caves and caverns. Sometimes the surface layer of rock becomes so thin that is collapses to produce a sinkhole. Many lakes are formed in this way.

Additionally, the fish and wildlife, which might be impacted by your dock project, are under the auspices of the Florida Game and Fresh Water Fish Commission.

Water levels are variable; thus, although the land you own ends at the established high water mark, your shoreline varies with high and low water times. Navigable rivers are owned by the state. Navigable waters and wetlands are also the responsibility of the U.S. Army Corps of Engineers. Navigable means there is a bed or a channel and enough water to support passage by a small craft. As a result, you normally cannot do anything which would restrict navigability, such as fence across the channel of a river or bay of the lake.

Rights and Responsibilities of the Property Owner

As the owner of the riparian (shoreline) area, you do have some privileges. These include exclusive right to the shoreline access to your lake, legal status to apply for permits for construction and change, and limited water use for lawn and garden watering. You also have the responsibility to take care of your property, be a good neighbor and citizen, and try to protect the lake on which you live. Consider joining or starting a Lake Association; together with your neighbors your can protect the value of your property and make your lake a better place to live.

Be Informed

Rules change and circumstances differ. Keep informed on state and local regulations and inquire before building anything, from a house to a dock or fence. This chapter provides a short introduction to the state and federal agencies whose regulatory responsibilities might be important to you as a lakefront

Rules change and circumstances differ. Keep informed on state and local regulations and inquire before building anything, from a house to a dock or fence.

property owner. See Chapter 13 for location maps of state and/or regional offices, addresses and phone numbers for state and federal agencies you might wish to contact for more information. ⁊

Did you know. . .

Did you know that the record largemouth bass recognized by the Florida Game and Fresh Water Fish Commission was caught in Big Fish Lake (a private lake) in Pasco County by Frederick Joseph "Fritz" Friebel in May, 1923? The fish weighed 20.13 lbs.!

CHAPTER 8

Federal, State, and Local Agencies

Federal, State, and Local Agencies

There are a number of federal, state, and local agencies whose responsibilities include wetlands and natural resources. Governments at all three levels have enacted laws and regulations which are enforced by these or other agencies.

A hierarchy of laws regulating aquatic resources exist, cascading from federal to state to local agencies. Each level can be more restrictive but not more lenient. We might, therefore, say that federal laws and regulations establish the "bottom line", followed by state and local regulations.

Being informed, then, means being aware of possible regulations at several levels and realizing that some activity, such as building a dock or altering the lakeshore, which might have been acceptable in another state, or even in another county or city in Florida, might not be legal in your area or on your lake.

Local governments, for example, may have canal districts (as in Winter Haven), conservation regulations (in Orange County for example), or establish boating or personal watercraft regulations which are more restrictive than those set by either federal or by state laws.

Because the law is complex and constantly changing and agency responsibilities may overlap, the information we can include here is only a beginning. In addition to the agencies listed in this chapter, Chapter 13 includes maps with locations of regional offices and addresses and phone numbers for those listed below.

Federal Agencies

U.S. Environmental Protection Agency (EPA). This agency sets regulations and standards, and enforces federal environmental pollution laws, delegating some of the permitting to state agencies (such as the DEP). The Clean Water Act and Safe Drinking Water Act are under its jurisdiction (see Chapter 5). The EPA also administers the Clean Lakes Program and encourages volunteer lake monitoring programs.

The EPA works closely with state agencies, providing money for programs and personnel. Here in Florida it has close ties with the DEP. It is organized by regions, with Florida a part of Region IV. (See Chapter 13 for our Regional office and national EPA offices and phone numbers.)

U.S. Army Corps of Engineers. The Corps of Engineers is responsible for activities in navigable waters and wetlands, especially relative to dredge and fill operations, under four related laws: the Rivers and Harbors Act of 1899, the Federal Water Pollution Control Act of 1972, the Clean Water Act of 1977, and the Marine Protection Research and Sanctuaries Act of 1972. Alterations

Federal Agencies

U.S. Environmental Protection Agency (EPA)

U.S. Army Corps of Engineers

U. S. Fish and Wildlife Service (FWS)

in wetlands, for example, some docks, riprap revetments and boat ramps, require permits. Contact your regional office (see Chapter 13) if you are planning activities which might fall under their jurisdiction.

U.S. Fish and Wildlife Service (FWS). This agency has the responsibility to protect wetlands, fish and wildlife resources, and endangered species. It oversees federal fish and wildlife programs authorized by several acts, including the Endangered Species Act and the Migratory Bird Act (see Chapter 13).

State of Florida Agencies

The legislature enacts "statutes" which provide the objectives and procedures to achieve them. These may be very specific but may also rely on the appropriate agencies to set the regulations by which the statutes will be interpreted and enforced.

To provide assurance that agencies will be fair in their enactment of these regulations, the State of Florida has enacted several laws which you should know about.

- The Florida Administrative Procedure Code (Chapter 120, Florida Statutes) guarantees that those affected by agency actions will be notified and that they have the right to be heard and to have input into the regulatory process.

- Florida Public Records Law (Chapter 119, Florida Statutes) makes agency records (with some exceptions) open to the public.

- Florida Sunshine Law (Chapter 286, Florida Statutes) makes meetings of governmental units where official actions are taken open to the public and requires that minutes be recorded.

State of Florida Agencies

Florida Game and Fresh Water Fish Commission (GFC)

Department of Environmental Protection (DEP)

Water Management Districts (WMD)

Department of Health and Rehabilitative Services (DHRS)

Most state agencies are similar in structure and have their headquarters in Tallahassee. There are also regional offices throughout the state. Use the Chapter 13 maps to determine which regional office has responsibility for your area. Each agency may have divisions according to responsibilities, such as permitting, enforcement, or education. The agency is headed either by a secretary or a cabinet officer or appointed commissioner. All agencies maintain close associations with the legislature to keep abreast of new laws or policies.

Florida Game and Fresh Water Fish Commission (GFC). This agency is responsible for managing, protecting and conserving wild animal life and fresh water aquatic life. It was created by Article IV, Section 9 of the 1968 Florida Constitution (F.A.C. Title 39). Habitat improvement, updating lists of species in need of protection, research, conservation information, and developing public recreation areas are some of its activities.

The GFC has jurisdiction over fresh water lakes and rivers; however, the Department of Environmental Protection has primary responsibility for water regulation enforcement, such as pollution regulation, public drinking water safety, administration of federal laws such as the Clean Water Act, and the permitting of dredging and filling in state waters. (Legal directives have given several agencies authority in the area of water regulations; hence, there is overlap in their activities.)

Department of Environmental Protection (DEP). This agency includes the former Dept.

Did you know...

Did you know that the water hyacinth (Eichhornia crassipes) *and frog's bit* (Limnobium spongia) *are often confused despite their differences. Frog's bit has small white flowers rather than showy lavender ones, white roots rather than dark, and spongy underleaf surfaces. Take a close look at them, the differences are easy to see. Does it have white flowers or white roots, or colored flowers and dark roots?*

of Natural Resources (created by the Florida Environmental Reorganization Act of 1975, F.A.C. Title 17) and the Dept. of Environmental Regulation (F.A.C. Title 9). The two agencies were combined on July 1, 1993. The responsibilities of the DEP include those from the two former agencies. In its broad role of regulating and protecting Florida's natural resources, it establishes standards and issues permits. The DEP, through separate agreements with each, delegates some of its water policy activities and permitting to the five water management districts. One of the DEP's divisions is the Bureau of Aquatic Plant Management. If your interest is in control of aquatic weeds or algae, start by contacting the regional office of this DEP division (see Chapter 13 for map and other information).

Water Management Districts (WMD). Florida has five water management districts which are responsible for surface and ground waters in their region. South Florida and Southwest Florida Water Management Districts were created by statute because of problems related to floods and water storage problems. The other three were created by the Florida Water Resources Act of 1972 (Chapter 373, Florida Statutes).

Each district is run by a governing board, which sets policies according to its powers. It is responsible for permits relative to wells, surface water management and storage, and water use within its area of jurisdiction. Some of the activities are delegated from the DEP. Recent efforts have attempted to coordinate the activities of the two groups through agreements

Did you know...

Did you know that Deep Lake in Collier County, which is over 50 meters deep, is considered one of Florida's deepest lakes? How different this lake is from Lake Okeechobee, the second largest lake completely within the United States and Florida's largest, which averages 2.7 meters in depth!

Of Tortoises and Men

Have you ever seen a big, brown, land turtle sitting on a mound next to a burrow, walking along, or crossing a road? Maybe there is one in your yard. Many people get great enjoyment from having a "resident tortoise"; others don't like the burrows they dig. This is typical behavior of the gopher tortoise, a threatened species in Florida and a familiar sight across the state. Now protected by law, the gopher tortoise was once collected for "turtle races" (often fund-raising events but banned in 1989), used as a source of food for people during the depression years (1930s), and often kept as backyard pets. Tortoises have specialized front feet for digging; their burrows are often six feet deep and may be over fifteen feet long. Gentle by nature, the tortoise can often be seen feeding on grasses, legumes, fruits, and berries during its daytime foraging excursions; it usually feeds within 50 feet of its burrow. These animals have been declining in number for some time despite their long life-span of 40 to 60 years. They are slow to mature and have small egg clutches, and the predation rate on hatchlings is high. They are important to the ecological balance of of xeric (dry) communities, partly because their burrows serve as homes for so many species of animals, including a number of other endangered species, the indigo snake for example. You can help by not collecting gopher tortoises (it's illegal anyway), not destroying their burrows, and preventing dogs from injuring them. You will be rewarded by the opportunity to observe a fascinating animal.

Joan Berish

(Source: Rare and Endangered Biota of Florida, Volume III by P.E. Moler, 1992, University Press of Florida, Gainesville, FL)

between the DEP and the WMDs. They also work together to implement the State Water Quality Plan with the DEP having the central responsibility of collecting information and data on water resources and assigning some permitting responsibilities to the WMDs.

Water management districts have the power to levy "ad valorem" (property) taxes in their district. There is a millage cap established by the Florida Constitution; millage rates are limited by statute.

Department of Health and Rehabilitative Services (DHRS). This agency has the responsibility to set up procedures to protect public health (F.A.C. Title 10). One of its responsibilities is to protect groundwater from sewage pollution. It issues permits for home sewage disposal systems and sets standards and regulations for placement relative to wells and surface waters.

For More Information...

Florida Wildlife Code, Title 39.
    Florida Game and Fresh Water Fish Commission. 1995. Tallahassee, Fla.
Handbook of Florida Water Regulation.
    by M.T. Olexa. 1991. Institute of Food and Agricultural Sciences, University of Florida.
    Gainesville, Fla. Florida Cooperative Extension Service Circular 1026.
Recognizing Wetlands.
    U.S. Army Corps of Engineers. Jacksonville, Fla.
Regulatory Program.
    U.S. Army Corps of Engineers. Jacksonville, Fla.
Rare and Endangered Biota of Florida, Volume III.
    by P.E. Moler, 1992. University Press of Florida, Gainesville, Fla. ❧

Wading birds forage in the shallow water of Paynes Prairie State Park.

CHAPTER 9

"Rules and Regs" — The Role of Local Government

...Zoning, regulations, and permits may be red tape,
but they also protect you and your lake.

As in many other activities, local governments, such as cities and counties, as well as state and federal agencies, regulate what you can do with and on lakefront property. Before you buy, before you build, and before you make changes to your shoreline or dock, find out what regulations the city or county might have and what permits you might need.

Regulation by City and County

Local government is the term that applies to city and county government. Within Florida there are a large number of different local governments. Many local governments regulate activities associated with owning and developing lakefront property. The activities regulated by local governments are in addition to the regulations administered by federal, regional, and state governments.

Although multiple levels of regulation may cause confusion, local government regulations pertaining to lakefront property provides certain benefits to the lakefront property owner. First, federal and state regulations tend to be broad in scope, not identifying specific water bodies and watersheds. Local government regulations on the other hand are often specific to a given lake or lakes within the jurisdiction of the local government. It is often the case that those rules administered by a local government will pertain only to your lake and the surrounding land. Second, as citizens generally contact their local government for assistance before contacting regional, state, and federal government, local government may be able to respond more quickly to your concerns than the other levels of government. Finally, where adequate regulations do not exist, it is more likely that a local government will develop the rule necessary to protect your particular lake and watershed.

Because requirements differ among local governments, it is important to know how they may affect you.

Because requirements differ among local governments, it is important to know how they may affect you. The following information identifies local government regulations pertaining to planning, growth management, and stormwater management. The last section of this chapter defines local programs. These are environmental programs conducted by various departments within many of our larger local governments throughout Florida, such as the City of Orlando.

Planning

Local governments throughout Florida are required by the State of Florida Growth Management Act to plan for growth. The purpose of this Act is to coordinate and direct growth throughout Florida. Local governments comply with the Act through implementing their respective Local Government Comprehensive Plans (LGCP). These plans have many elements that include land use, housing, transportation, economic development, recreation, and conservation.

Depending on where you live in Florida, the Future Land Use Element and the Conservation Element of each LGCP serve to guide land usage around your lake and within its watershed. These elements may contain rules pertaining to setback distances from the water's edge, density limitations within the watershed, and may define permissible uses of land within the watershed.

Because use of the land around your lake will affect your enjoyment and use, land use planning by local government can be either beneficial or detrimental to the lakefront property owner. Should you have questions pertaining to land use planning and restrictions, contact your local government's planning department or the Regional Planning Council in your area.

Land Development Regulations

Local governments manage their growth through specific Land Development regulations. These regulations govern development and land usage. Land Development regulations may restrict certain activities within a watershed while permitting other activities. Examples of restricted activities include prohibiting development within wetlands, flood zones, and designated conservation areas. Typical permitted activities include the building of boat docks, piers and retaining walls, some dredging and filling activities, and lakeshore plant removal.

Land Development regulations are intended to manage growth. Because growth that occurs around your lake and within its watershed may affect your enjoyment, Land Development regulations can protect lakefront property owners from detrimental growth. Before you or your neighbors conduct any construction-related activities around your lake, you should check with your local government's land development department.

Should you have questions pertaining to land use planning and restrictions, contact your local government's planning department or the Regional Planning Council in your area.

Stormwater

Stormwater runoff is the term that applies to water flowing over buildings, streets, and the land's surface during and immediately after a rainstorm. Excessive stormwater runoff may cause flooding. Stormwater runoff also carries pollutants that could degrade surface water quality.

Many local governments have programs and regulations pertaining to the management of stormwater runoff. Some local governments administer a stormwater utility program which funds the management of stormwater. The purpose of these programs and regulations is to minimize the chance of flooding and to reduce pollution. Stormwater regulations typically specify methods for the storage and treatment of stormwater before it is released to municipal storm sewers and surface waters

Because stormwater management practices depend on local weather patterns, land use, and physiography (natural features of the earth's surface), local governments have a vital role in stormwater management. Contact your local government's stormwater management department should you have any questions. If you live in an area where the local government does not have a stormwater management department, contact your public works department.

Local Programs

Many local governments in Florida administer their own environmental programs. These programs, which are commonly referred to as local programs, may include surface water quality, stormwater, groundwater, air quality and environmental permitting, boating activities, and speed limits. These programs are staffed with professionals who are available to answer your questions. Some of the larger local governments even have lake management

Mark Brenner

Water was diverted into Lake Brooklyn in 1994.

professionals who can provide assistance. These local programs may be able to provide information specific to your lake, collect and analyze water samples, supply you with information specific to your lake, investigate water quality problems, and answer questions for you or your homeowners association.

Some programs have professionals that provide presentations to homeowners associations as well as civic groups. Where homeowners associations do not exist, your local government may have a neighborhood service department which can assist in setting up a lake homeowners association. Lake owners associations usually have their own rules and regulations which may be even more restrictive than those at governmental levels.

You should be able to determine whether your local government administers a local program by contacting one or more of the following departments: Planning, Environmental Management/Protection, Growth Management, Stormwater, Public Works, Engineering and/or Water and Sewer. These departments are also responsible for administering various environmental regulations pertaining to planning, growth management and stormwater.

If your local government does not have professionals or programs that can help, you may want to contact the Florida Lake Management Society for suggestions on where to look for assistance.

If your local government does not have professionals or programs that can help, you may want to contact the Florida Lake Management Society for suggestions on where to look for assistance. Simply address a letter in care of "President — Florida Lake Management Society" and mail it to the address provided in this book. ❧

CHAPTER 10

Water: Protection and Regulation

As a limited resource in an expanding population, water, its use and its supply, is regulated and protected. This is important to you, not only as a citizen with a need for a clean and safe water supply, but as a lakefront property owner with a vested interest in the waterbody at your doorstep. Therefore, we have included here a brief introduction to some of the major laws directed to this objective and the types of activities which are regulated because they affect our surface and ground waters.

The Clean Water Act (CWA)

This federal law was enacted by Congress in 1970 to protect all waters subject to tides, which cross state boundaries or are important in interstate or foreign commerce. In addition to the marine environments, this law includes wetlands and any rivers or waterbodies which have any connection to commerce beyond state boundaries.

The Clean Water Act limits pollutants through enforcement of discharge permitting regulations. It is primarily enforced through the U.S. EPA.

(However, dredge and fill operations are the responsibility of the U.S. Army Corps of Engineers.) This is done through permits which specify the amounts of pollutants which can be discharged, the schedule of discharge, and mandates testing procedures. The EPA sets standards relative to pollutants; the state can also set standards, which must be at least as tough as the federal ones. The EPA may delegate permitting processes to the state.

The Clean Water Act requires "point source" polluters to get permits. Any pipe, ditch, or anything emptying or draining pollutants into a particular area is a point source. Non-point sources, except for agricultural stormwater run-off and irrigation system return drainage, now also need a permit. Municipalities with populations over 100,000 must obtain NPDES non-point source permits to regulate urban stormwater runoff. Levels are set dependent upon the content of the pollutant relative to the ability of present technology to treat it and the type of water body it will affect (water quality).

What does the Clean Water Act have to do with an individual lakefront property owner? The permitting process for point source pollution is aimed primarily at industry. However, it may help in protecting your lake if you have lake problems which may result from some type of point source pollution.

Comprehensive Environmental Response, Compensation, and Liability Act (CERCLA)

This act, referred to as CERCLA or Superfund, was passed by Congress in 1980 to provide funds to investigate and clean up sites contaminated with hazardous substances. This is enforced by the EPA, which has a list of substances involved. It ordinarily should have little relevance to you as an individual lakefront property owner. However, in the unlikely event that you have purchased land in which hazardous materials had been buried, even if the

What does the Clean Water Act have to do with an individual lakefront property owner?

. . .

...it may help in protecting your lake if you have lake problems which may result from some type of point source pollution.

contamination occurred prior to your purchase and you had no knowledge of it, you could be liable for cleanup. A check on the past history of the land prior to purchase should prevent this problem.

Safe Drinking Water Act (SDWA)

This law was enacted in 1974 to protect the public's drinking water supply. Its purpose was to establish standards for drinking water, monitor public water systems and protect groundwater against deep injection wells. If you are on a municipal water system, this law, administered and enforced by the state under EPA, protects your drinking water. It also could be important to you and your lake if there are injection wells in your vicinity which could contaminate the groundwater.

The State of Florida, as in most states today, handles regulation and enforcement of the SDWA. Through a 1986 amendment, the EPA retains the right to enforce water quality violations if the state does not.

Federal Insecticide, Fungicide, and Rodenticide Act

Originally enacted by Congress in the 1940s, this law was amended in 1988 to include all activities involving pesticides, from sale to disposal. Organisms which the EPA defines as pests fall under this act.

All pesticides must be registered with the EPA and labeled relative to contents, uses, and warnings. Some, classified as general-use pesticides, can be applied by anyone and

Did you know...

Did you know that Long Pond, south of Chiefland in Levy County, is unusual because it is a sinkhole lake that resulted from sinks forming along a fault line. The fault, or crack in the underlying rock, allows the eroding water to form an elongated rather than a circular sink.

require no permit. Restricted-use pesticides require you to be state-certified to get a permit to buy or apply them (or to hire a commercial applicator). These pesticides are restricted because if used improperly they could pose a danger to either the operator or the environment. The State of Florida, under cooperative agreements with the EPA, trains and certifies pesticide applicators. Florida also has passed additional laws covering pesticide use, with enforcement by the Dept. of Agriculture and Consumer Services (DACS). See Chapter 13 for contact information.

Aquatic plants and aquatic plant management are included in this law. Before you take any action to control aquatic plants in your lake, contact the Bureau of Aquatic Plant Management of the DEP for your region (see Chapter 13). In addition to any herbicide permit you might need, this will insure that your proposed solution does not violate any state regulations protecting aquatic plants and the lake itself (see Chapter 4 for more information).

Endangered Species Act (ESA)

This law was passed by Congress in 1974 to protect wild animals and plants which are threatened with extinction and also the ecosystems which they need to live. This means that when endangered species are being protected, lakes often are also protected.

The Endangered Species Act restricts your ability to collect, hunt, or otherwise harass or destroy species which may be on your land or lake. For example, keeping these animals as pets, collecting protected plants, or removing gopher tortoises from your land are all illegal. States, as Florida has, may put further restrictions on species which may not be on the federal list but are in danger here. Some species, such as the American alligator, are now off the list and are hunted with special permits and quotas.

Before you take any action to control aquatic plants in your lake, contact the Bureau of Aquatic Plant Management of the DEP for your region.

National Environmental Policy Act (NEPA)

NEPA was passed in 1969 and amended in 1975. It encourages "harmony between man and his environment", to prevent or eliminate environmental damage and to increase "understanding of ecological systems and natural resources". Under NEPA, proposed federal action must be examined "to determine its effect on the human environment".

The "NEPA Process" involves public hearings, drafting an Environmental Assessment, public hearings to determine whether an Environmental Impact Statement is needed. (If not, preparing a "Finding of no Significant Impact" draft for agency and public response is necessary prior to any action.)

More Laws?

We have included here a few of the more important federal laws pertaining to water and waterbodies. However, the State of Florida also has many laws and regulations enacted to protect our water supply, our fresh and salt-water ecosystems and our wildlife. These laws may duplicate federal laws, be more restrictive, or cover specifics which the broader act may not include. Responsibility for enforcement lies with one or more of our state agencies. There may in turn be additional local regulations.

For example, regulations involving water wells involve both the DEP and the water management districts. Sewage systems are under the jurisdiction of the Dept. of Health and Rehabilitative Services. Construction or repair of either involve use of licensed contractors (who will be aware of any local regulations and restrictions) and permits from the appropriate agency.

Throughout this chapter, we include references to regulations, their enforcing agencies, and who to contact whenever we think they are important to you as a lakefront property owner. ⋙

Before you leave...read the rules.

CHAPTER 11

Recreational Laws and Regulations 1: Boating for Pleasure and Safety

Thomas Wright

…Be safe and considerate!

People buy property on lakes for a variety of reasons: to gain access to the water for boating or swimming, to enjoy the aesthetics of living on the water, or to enjoy a close association with wildlife. If you enjoy boating, whether canoeing, sailing, motorboating, or jetskiing, you need to know about local, state, and federal boating regulations regarding registration, safety and consideration for others. If you have a lake association, work together to make sure your active recreation, such as boating, also allows you and others quiet enjoyment of waterfront living and does not degrade sensitive environmental areas.

So, you now are a waterfront property owner. You either have a boat which came with the property or you have acquired one. Before you take it out for a spin and meet the local Wildlife Officer, there are things you need to know.

Do You Know?

There are federal, state and local use, equipment and safety regulations which apply to recreational boats and boating. You need to know what they are! (These rules and regulations are always changing, so you also have to keep up with these changes.)

Current rules and regulations include:

- Your boat, unless it is not motor-powered, needs to be registered and/or numbered to operate in Florida waters. Exceptions may include those operating only on "private" lakes (subject to definition of "private") or ponds and those which have a current number from another state or country and are here fewer than 90 days. Most also must be titled in Florida.

- All boats must have at least one U.S. Coast Guard approved personal flotation device (PFD) per passenger. Boats 16 feet or longer must have one for every passenger plus one throwable device.

- Florida law requires that every child under 6 must wear a PFD aboard any vessel under 26 feet while "underway."

- You should have at least one B-1-type approved hand portable fire extinguisher on your motorboat. (Check for other stipulations.)

- Operating a motorboat while intoxicated is both a federal and state offense and may be subject to fine or imprisonment and points against your driver's license.

- A flashing blue light indicates a law enforcement boat; you should slow your speed, yield right-of-way or stop your boat, if necessary.

Operating a motorboat while intoxicated is both a federal and state offense and may be subject to fine or imprisonment and points against your driver's license.

- Two flags in the water or on boats indicate the presence of divers. The first one, Alpha, is internationally recognized as indicating diving operations, and vessels displaying it should be given the right-of-way. The second, red with a white diagonal stripe, is required by Florida law. Never approach within 100 feet of any object or boat with either flag.

- Low-level and conventional dams are dangerous to boaters. Watch for markers and stay clear, both above and below the dam.

- If you operate your boat in a "negligent" manner by endangering lives or property, you are subject to fine or imprisonment. Examples are boating in a swimming area or excessive speed near other boats.

- Be alert for "manatee zones." If you cannot avoid their habitats, watch for them, stay at idle or no-wake speed and in the center of the channel. Careless boaters are the major enemy of manatees.

- Channel 16 VHF-FM is a calling and distress channel which you can use if you need help.

The State of Florida, through the Florida Game and Fresh Water Fish Commission (GFC) and the Florida Marine Patrol (FMP), publishes a "Boater's Guide" available through your local tag agency, which will provide you with important legal and safety information.

Contact the GFC or the FMP (Florida Marine Patrol) for information on their free boating safety courses (See Chapter 13 for addresses). You can also call 1-800-366-BOAT for information on free boating courses given by the U.S. Coast Guard Auxiliary and other agencies.

You can also call 1-800-366-BOAT for information on free boating courses given by the U.S. Coast Guard Auxiliary and other agencies.

If you are under 16, you are required to complete a boating safety course in order to operate a watercraft with an engine greater than 10 horsepower. Each year this age requirement will rise incrementally until, by the year 2001, everyone under 21 will be required to complete a boating safety course.

If you plan to fish, you will probably need a Florida license (see Chapter 12 on Fishing for a few exceptions). You can now get a 5-year fishing license for both freshwater and saltwater fishing. For information on cost and where to purchase your license, call the Florida Game and Fresh Water Fish Commission at (904) 488-3641.

Federal Regulations

Recreational boaters are subject to federal laws, equipment requirements, and safety regulations. These are discussed in the pamphlet from the U.S. Coast Guard listed at the end of the chapter and available at your local tag agency. Regulations vary by size of boat and size and type of waters. Manatees are protected by federal law, the U.S. Marine Mammal Protection Act, and the Endangered Species Act.

Federal law requires that all boating accidents in which someone dies or disappears be reported to the nearest state boating authority. For more information, you can call the Boating Safety Hotline, 1-800-368-5647.

State Regulations

Florida has adopted the federal regulations regarding safety equipment to be carried on a boat. Minimum required equipment depends on boat class:

- One approved back-fire arrester
- Ventilation equipment
- Personal flotation devices: one per person on board or being towed

Small children should always wear a life vest specifically approved for children.

- Bell whistle
- Visual distress signals
- Fire extinguisher

Specific requirements for boat type and size classes are given in the "Florida Boater's Guide." See "For More Information" at the end of this chapter.

All engines on all boats must be reasonably muffled when operated anywhere in the state. This includes personal watercraft and airboats.

Florida has also adopted as law the U.S. Coast Guard Navigation Rules. These require everyone to "conduct his vessel in a prudent manner, at a safe speed, constantly maintaining a proper lookout by all means available to him." Rules relating to sound signals, crossing, overtaking, and what to do during restricted visibility are discussed in the "Boater's Guide." Be sure you are familiar with them.

There is a uniform State and Federal Waterway Marking System with which you should be familiar. On state waters, red and green buoys mark channel limits and are usually in pairs. The boat should pass between the red and green pair. Since the buoys may not always be in pairs, just remember to keep the red one on the right as you come in ("Red on right returning"). Other markers are regulatory.

The law allows an enforcement officer to stop and board boats to check for compliance with federal or state law. The boat can be made to return to the closest dock until any hazardous condition is corrected. In additon to the equipment required for safety listed above, other factors, such as overloading, leaking fuel, excessive water leakage, and fuel accumulation are especially hazardous.

Marilyn D. Bachmann

Boaters return from a day spent fishing on the lake.

The Big Switch

Scientists are learning that shallow lakes don't always behave the same as deep lakes. For example, Florida has many shallow lakes with abundant nutrients. Such lakes should be filled with greenish water, but they have clear water because much of the surface area is covered with aquatic macrophytes (plants). This plant cover can be lost during very high water, or if a storm tears it up, after herbicide treatment or the addition of grass carp. Without the plants, the water may become turbid and look like pea soup due to algae and, sometimes, resuspended bottom sediments. A clear-water, macrophyte lake tends to stay the way it is, and a turbid, algal lake will remain green and turbid unless something happens to cause a switch. A drought which lowers the lake level and allows the plants to return may switch a turbid, algal lake back to a clear-water, macrophyte lake. Lake biologists call this "Alternative Stable States" in which the lake can switch states without any change in the external nutrient supply to the lake.

Secchi disk shows clear water in a macrophyte-filled lake.

Clear water shows between patches of macrophytes in a lake.

The state also says:

- Oil cannot be discharged into navigable waters, nor should it be pumped into the bilge of the boat.

- Trash must not be disposed of on beaches, marshes, or overboard.

- You cannot moor to any buoy except mooring buoys.

- Manatees are protected by the Florida Manatee Sanctuary Act which established over 20 manatee protection zones in Florida where boat speed is limited.

- Personal watercraft ("jet skis") are considered power boats and must follow the same navigation rules as larger boats. These include observing swimming areas and no-wake zones. It is against the law to alter the muffling equipment — it is both illegal and inconsiderate to others. If you are using a jet ski, you must: wear a PFD; operate only during the day; have the kill switch lanyard attached to yourself; and be 14 or older (16 or older to operate a rented craft).

- Waterskiing is prohibited from one half hour after sunset to one half hour before sunrise. Either a rear view mirror or a second person is required on board the tow craft to watch the skier.

- Races, regattas, and other marine events must be reported to authorities (county sheriff, Florida Game and Fresh Water Fish Commission, or the Florida Marine Patrol) at least 15 days before the event.

- In Florida, speed is limited under certain conditions. Comply with posted signs and be aware of local city and county regulations. Always operate at a speed which will not endanger others.

Children should always wear personal flotation devices (PFDs) when boating.

- By Florida law, driving a boat while drunk carries heavy fines, imprisonment, non-paid public service work, and mandatory substance abuse counseling. Sentencing is mandatory. The law also says that if you operate a vehicle, you "consent to chemical testing of breath, blood, or urine." Operating a vehicle while intoxicated is also a federal offense.

Other state requirements, including registration, numbering, applying for a title, and safety regulations are discussed in the "Boater's Guide," as are tips for safe boating and trailering. Courtesy examinations by the Marine Patrol or wildlife officer are available to be sure all boats have the required equipment. The U.S. Coast Guard Auxiliary conducts a courtesy marine exam (CME) and gives you a CME decal if you meet the requirement; the decal may help you get an insurance discount.

Local Ordinances

Be sure to check with your local government for regulations about boating which may be in addition to state and federal regulations. Usually these have to do with speed limits, motor size, no motors, restricted areas, or waterskiing time limits.

The Ol' Swimmin' Hole

For many people, one of the great pleasures of living on a lake is swimming; this is one reason that clear lakes with sand bottoms have high real estate values. Florida's warm waters make this possible for many months of the year. Many safety considerations related to swimming are the same in southern and northern lakes. However, others, such as relate to the presence of alligators, are new to people who have moved to Florida from northern states.

For many people, one of the great pleasures of living on a lake is swimming; this is one reason that clear lakes with sand bottoms have high real estate values.

Swimmers vs. Watercraft. Safety precautions for swimmers include not swimming alone or in unfamilar areas. Swim in areas marked or roped off to keep boats away or stay close to shore and out of the path of boat traffic. However, even when you are near shore always be aware of motorized craft. Personal watercraft riders and water-skiers often come closer to shore than they should, and accidents can happen, even near docks.

Swimmers and Gators. In Florida, you must be alert for alligators, especially in green water and dark water lakes, where they are more difficult to see. They may be basking along the shore, floating in the water or under shelters, such as docks. While they normally are not particularly aggressive, it is wisest not to swim where they are (see Chapter 3 on wildlife for more information).

"Look before you leap." Every year, accidents happen because people swim or dive in waters with hazards unknown to them. Some of these have already been discussed. A good safety precaution is to become familiar with the lake, river, or beach area where you intend to swim. Know where the drop-offs are, and whether there are currents that could put you at risk. Swim and dive only in areas where you can see the bottom and any possible hazards. Paying attention to good swimming practices, such as never swimming alone and being familiar with your "swimmin' hole," can help you and your family enjoy a safe and fun recreational activity.

Did you know...

Did you know that anyone born after September 30, 1980 must have successfully completed a boating safety course and be able to prove it before they can operate a motorized watercraft 10 hp or greater. This law will be phased in until October 1, 2001, when everyone 21 or younger will be included under this law. Details about this and other boating regulations can be found at the Web site http://boatsafe.com/ Florida/

Be Safe and Be Considerate!

Always think about your own safety and the safety of others when operating or riding in a boat. Today's "fun" or practical joke can become tomorrow's tragedy. Be considerate; don't take your boat into areas where people are swimming, slow down near people fishing, don't engage in noisy activities or motor boating late in evening. Help make your lake safe and enjoyable for everyone. Potentially conflicting lake uses can coexist when we think about what we are doing and our effect on other people.

When a Hurricane is Coming!

There are recommended procedures for protection of life and property when a hurricane is headed your way. If you have a boat or own a marina, there are additional protective measures that should be taken. See "Recommendations for Hurricane Preparation and Response for Boating Communities and Industries" listed below.

Overregulation?

Does it seem that watercraft regulations are overdone? Maybe, but with three quarters of a million registered boats and personal watercraft and more boating-related accidents than any other state in 1996, laws and regulations help to make Florida waters a safer place for all of us.

Always think about your own safety and the safety of others when operating or riding in a boat.

For More Information...

For further information on basic safety requirments, check with your local wildlife officer or Marine Patrol officer.

Contact either your nearest regional office of the Florida Game and Fresh Water Fish Commission or Florida Marine Patrol district office for boating safety courses.

Obtain the most recent editions of the following three publications, available through your local office of the Florida Department of Motor Vehicles:

A Guide to Safe and Efficient Recreational Boating in Florida.
> by D.G. Cook. 1992. Institute of Food and Agricultural Sciences, University of Florida. Gainesville, Fla. Florida Cooperative Extension Service Fact Sheet EES-68.

Federal Requirements and Safety Tips for Recreational Boats.
> U.S. Coast Guard, U.S. Department of Transportation. Washington, DC.

Florida Boater's Guide: A Guide to Safety Afloat.
> Florida Game and Fresh Water Fish Commission, Florida Marine Patrol. Tallahassee, Fla.

Recommendations for Hurricane Preparation and Responses for Boating Communities and Industries.
> Institute of Food and Agricultural Science, University of Florida. Gainesville, Fla. Florida Cooperative Extension Service Publication TP-75.

Sailboats and Lightning.
> Florida Sea Grant, Institute of Food and Agricultural Sciences, University of Florida. Gainesville, Fla. Florida Cooperative Extension Service videotape SGEB-17.

The Disaster Handbook–1998 National Edition.
> 1998. Institute of Food and Agricultural Sciences, University of Florida. Gainesville, Fla. Florida Cooperative Extension Service publication SP-241. ❧

Jet skis are fun but are not permitted on all lakes.

CHAPTER 12

Recreational Laws and Regulations 2: Fishing and Hunting

To live off the land isn't the goal of most people who enjoy fishing or hunting, but there is a little bit of that feeling in sitting down to a panfish dinner or having wild turkey for Thanksgiving.

Fishing

To live on a lake means increased opportunities to "catch the big one" for the dedicated fisherman or perhaps enjoy the quiet and relaxation of fishing.

Florida has some of the greatest warmwater fishing in the world. With the diversity offered by over 7000 lakes, as well as many rivers, and other wetlands, fishing in Florida has a lot to offer, and you, as a waterfront property owner, are on the "front lines." However, before you go out there and put that line in the water, you may need a license and you do need to know the fishing regulations.

The Florida Game and Fresh Water Fish Commission has the responsibility "to manage our freshwater aquatic life and wild animal life and their

habitats." This means preserving, restoring, and managing habitat as well as populations for "optimum sustained use." To help carry out this responsibility, this agency establishes and enforces fishing regulations which are updated annually and are available to you at your local tag agency; ask for the current edition of the Freshwater Sport Fishing Guide and Regulations Summary.

If you are interested in information on saltwater fishing, call the Florida Dept. of Environmental Protection. For freshwater fishing, some of the more important and general information is listed here. For more detail and to keep up with the annual changes, make sure you obtain a copy of the "Regulations Summary." Also, you can always get information and up-to-date fishing regulations by calling 1-800-ASK-FISH. Unless otherwise stated, we assume you are a Florida resident.

Do You Need a License? You will need a license if you are over 16 and under 65. A license can be obtained from your county tax collector or sub-agents at stores which sell tackle and sporting goods or at fishing camps. You must carry the license with you when fishing. People 65 or older and those disabled must carry either a Senior Citizen Certificate or Permanent Hunting and Fishing Certificate; these are free of charge from county tax collectors.

There are some exceptions to the license requirment. For example, you don't need a license if you are totally and permanently disabled. Also, the Cane Pole law exempts you from needing a license in your county of residence if you fish with a cane pole or line only (no reel), use live or natural bait, and do not fish for commercial purposes. However, you will need a license to fish in any lake designated as a Fish Management Area, regardless of your fishing method.

Randy Meyers

A big catch!

LIVING AT THE LAKE

You can now order your fishing license by calling a toll-free number: 1-888-FISH-FLORIDA (1-888-347-4356). With a major credit card, you will be issued an instant temporary license. The permanent one will be mailed within 48 hours. These numbers and information about licenses as well as other information are available on the Florida Game and Fresh Water Fish Commission Web site: http://sun6.dms.state.fl.us/gfc

License fees are set by the Florida Legislature and may change. Residents may purchase annual, 5-year, or lifetime licenses. Non-residents may purchase licenses for 12 months, 7 days, or 3 days. Lifetime fishing and Sportsman's licenses are also available; the cost depends upon your age. A Sportsman's license combines hunting and fishing priveleges.

Lifetime Licenses. Since price is based on age, the earlier you purchase a lifetime license to fish in Florida, the more you will save. You may find this a good option for your children or grandchildren. These licenses are valid even if you later move out of Florida. You can get a license for freshwater fishing only or a Lifetime Sportsman's for hunting and fishing (salt- and freshwater). See the Regulations Summary for included activities.

Home Sweet Home. You and your family do not need a license to fish from your own property ("homestead"). However, this applies only if you are on the shore; if you go out in a boat, have a license.

Did you know...

Did you know the Florida Game and Fresh Water Fish Commission has a "Big Catch Program". If your fish is above a certain weight (for example, a largemouth bass over 10 lbs.) you will be certified in the "Big Catch Program" and receive a signed certificate. Depending upon the number and species of fish which qualified as "Big Catches", you can get an award as a "Specialist", "Master" or "Elite" Angler and get your name on the GFC website as well (http//fcn.state.fl.us/gfc/fishing/bigcatch/bigcatch.html).

Private Fishing Ponds. You may fish without a license in a private fishing pond if it is less than 20 acres in size. A private fishing pond is one which is manmade for fishing purposes and is not connected to other surface waters. If you own a private fishing pond larger than 20 acres, you may purchase a license on a per acre basis which permits you to allow any person to fish on it without a license. You, as the homestead owner, and your spouse and minor children do not need a license to fish on a pond within your own homestead.

Know Your Fish. Seasons, sizes, and bag limits vary for different species of fish. So, you need to be able to recognize the species of fish you might catch. This also applies to some kinds of saltwater fish, even if you are fishing in fresh waters. Saltwater fish can be caught in freshwater rivers and in some lakes, like Lake George, but you cannot keep them if you do not have a salt-water fishing license, even if they are caught in season. So learn to recognize such fish as snook, redfish, and mullet, in case you hook one. Conversely, if you are fishing in brackish water with a saltwater license, you might encounter a largemouth bass, which requires a freshwater fishing license!

You also need to know which fish are considered game and which are nongame fish. There are publications, such as "Fishing Inside Florida" (see below), which include fish identification drawings in addition to maps and other information.

Freshwater Fishing Regulations. Fishing regulations include restrictions on how and when you catch the fish, what types of bait you can use, how you catch your bait, length limits, and bag limits. These regulations may differ from lake to lake. For example, in fresh water, you may not take fish while swimming or diving. Other restricted methods include explosives, firearms, poison, electricity, or spear guns. You may not sell or transport fish out of the state except that licensed fishermen may take two days' bag limit of legally

Seasons, sizes, and bag limits vary for different species of fish. So, you need to be able to recognize the species of fish you might catch.

harvested game fish. See the Regulations Summary for special regulations for Fish Management Areas and lakes which may have special restrictions. For these areas, there are both general regulations and special regulations for specific waterbodies. These are listed for you, by region, in the Regulations Summary.

Fish and Mercury. Some of Florida's freshwater locations have been tested for mercury and have been given a health advisory status. These lakes and ponds, management areas, national parks, and wildlife refuges are given a status of "unrestricted consumption," "limited consumption," or "no consumption." Individual lakes and their health advisory status are listed by name in the Regulations Summary.

Hunting

There are many opportunities for hunting in Florida. Perhaps this is one of your particular interests or maybe you bought waterfront property with some acreage in a rural area. If you intend to hunt only on your own property, you will not need a license. Anyone born after June 1, 1975, must take the Hunter Safety Course offered each year in every county by the Florida Game and Fresh Water Fish Commission.

You can get a resident game hunting license for one year or a Sportsman's license (or Lifetime Sportsman's license) which combines hunting with both fresh- and saltwater fishing. An additional license is needed to take fur-bearing animals such as nutria or raccoon. Depending upon your interest, you may also need one or more of the following stamps: waterfowl stamp (plus a federal duck stamp), archery, muzzle-loader, game management area, and turkey — all of these are included under the Sportsman's license. For license fees and specific regulations and requirements, pick up the current "Hunting

Ducks migrate south and winter on Florida lakes.

Handbook Regulations Summary" when you get your license (available from county tax collectors or subagents at sporting goods stores).

Unprotected Animals. There are a few animals which are not protected by either state or federal law. Unproteceted birds include English sparrows, Muscovy ducks, European starlings, and rock doves (pigeons). Muscovies are exotics, and many local governments consider them nuisances, like pigeons, and therefore, prohibit citizens from collecting, purchasing, or releasing these birds. Some cities have responded to citizens who like Muscovy ducks and have established protections for them. Migratory nongame birds which are causing damage may be taken under permit. Examples of such birds are blackbirds, cowbirds, crows, and grackles.

Unprotected animals include the armadillo, coyote, Norway rat, black rat, and house mouse. In most parts of Florida, wild hogs are not considered native animals and can be taken on private property with the landowner's permission. You can take frogs by a variety of methods and most freshwater turtles without a license throughout the year, but only for noncommercial purposes.

Leave 'Em Alone. You need to be aware of protected species. Your regional Florida Game and Fresh Water Fish Commission office can supply a current list of species that are either endangered, threatened, or of special concern.

Native birds are protected by state and federal law and can be taken only in accordance with regulations indicated in the "Hunting Handbook Regulations Summary." You cannot take deer by any method in the Florida Keys of Monroe County. Several aquatic turtles and the gopher tortoise are protected and may not be taken, sold, or possessed. Alligators may be harvested only by special permit in certain areas.

You need to be aware of protected species. Your regional Florida Game and Fresh Water Fish Commission office can supply a current list of species that are either endangered, threatened, or of special concern.

Wildlife Law Violations. If you see someone violating Florida's wildlife laws, such as shooting from a roadway or killing and selling wildlife, you can report this through the toll-free Wildlife Alert hotline. This connects you to a regional office of the GFC from which officers can be dispatched.

Wildlife Alert Hotline

To report wildlife law violations:

Panama City	1-800-342-1676
Lake City	1-800-342-8105
Ocala	1-800-342-9620
Lakeland	1-800-282-8002
West Palm Beach	1-800-432-2046

For More Information...

Fishing Inside Florida Directory, 3d edition.
　　by Roger Bellamy. 1988. Hillsboro Publishing Co., P.O. Box 1657, Tampa, Fla. 33601.
Freshwater Sport Fishing Guide and Regulations Summary.
　　Florida Game and Fresh Water Fish Commission. Tallahassee, Fla. Annual publication. Call 1-800-ASK-FISH for up-to-date regulations and information.
Hunting Handbook Regulations Summary.
　　Florida Game and Fresh Water Fish Commission. Tallahassee, Fla. Annual publication.
Florida Wildlife.
　　Florida Game and Fresh Water Fish Commission. Tallahassee, Fla. Bimonthly.
1998-99 Florida Wildlife Code, Title 39.
　　Florida Game and Fresh Water Fish Commission. Tallahassee, Fla.
Mercury, Largemouth Bass, and Water Quality: A Preliminary Report.
　　by J. Hand and M. Friedman. 1990. Department of Environmental Protection. Tallahassee, Fla.
Handbook of Common Freshwater Fish in Florida Lakes.
　　by M.V. Hoyer and D.E. Canfield, Jr. 1995. Institute of Food and Agricultural Sciences, University of Florida. Gainesville, Fla. Florida Cooperative Extension Service publication SP-160. 178 pp.
Handbook of Florida Water Regulation.
　　by M.T. Olexa. 1991. Institute of Food and Agricultural Sciences, University of Florida. Gainesville, Fla. Florida Cooperative Extension Service Circular 1026. ❧

Record catches are found in Florida lakes.

Mark V. Foyer

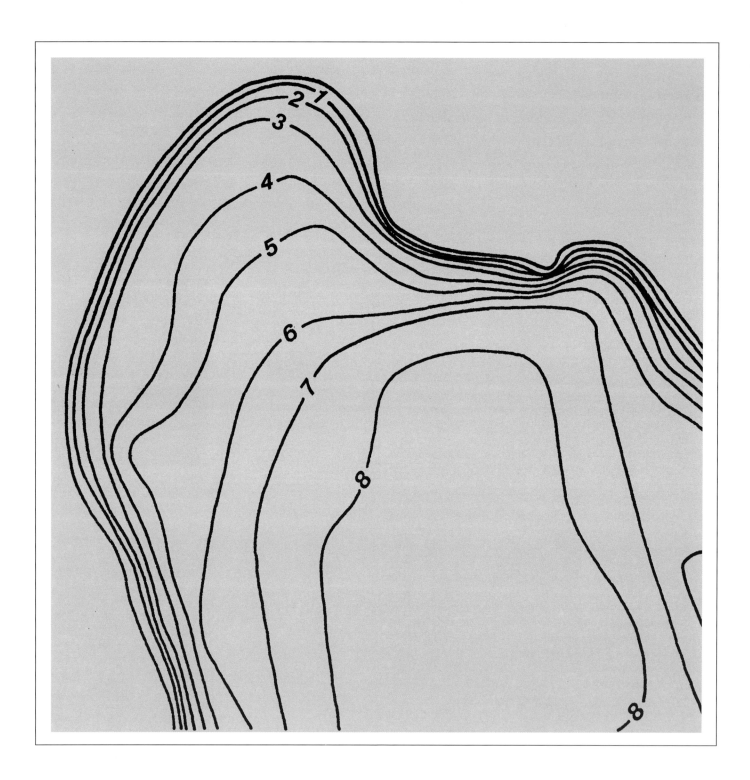

CHAPTER 13

Maps & Addresses of Organizations & Agencies Concerned with Fresh Water & Waterbodies

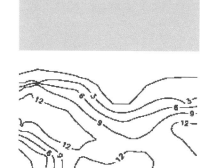

In this chapter, we provide you with information on the agencies and organizations concerned with water and waterbody welfare and regulation. Brief descriptions, addresses, and maps showing territories of regional offices are given in three broad categories:

I. University of Florida including Institute for Food and Agricultural Sciences (UF/IFAS), Cooperative Extension Service, and Florida LAKEWATCH

II. Agencies of the State of Florida

III. Federal Agencies

Local/Regional Management Contacts:

Use the space below for the names of your local contacts for lake management concerns.

_____

DEP District Lake Management Coordinator

_____

Water Management District Contact

_____

Regional Game and Fresh Water Fish Commission Biologist

_____

DEP Bureau of Aquatic Plant Control Biologist

_____

Univ. of Florida County Extension Agent

_____

City or Town Council President

_____

Country Commission Chair

_____

Zoning Administrator

_____

Local Planning Administrator

_____

Your Lake Association or District Contact Person

Florida has many agencies to help you when you are considering spending your life living on a lake.

I. University of Florida

University of Florida Institute of Food and Agricultural Sciences (UF/IFAS), Gainesville, FL

Research and education on issues related to natural resources throughout the state of Florida, including water quality. Educational publications and videos available. IFAS has also made this information available on the World Wide Web (http://edis.ifas.ufl.edu). IFAS includes the Cooperative Extension Service which has offices in every county throughout the state.

UF/IFAS Cooperative Extension Service

In addition to major state programs which provide information and assistance to the people of Florida, Extension makes available numerous fact sheets, bulletins, and other publications as a service to the public. Many of these publications are useful to the lakefront property owner and are listed in the "For more information" section at the end of each chapter in this book. Visit your county Extension office (see below) for copies of these publications as well as advice and other assistance. You also can access information about the county Extension offices, including addresses, phone numbers and even maps to help you find the offices on the World Wide Web (http://www.ifas.ufl.edu).

A scenic boardwalk crosses a shallow area at the edge of Lake Wauberg.

Fla. Dept. of Env. Protection

County Extension Offices

Alachua County Extension Office
2800 NE 39 Avenue
Gainesville, FL 32609-2658
(352) 955-2402

Baker County Extension Office
Route 3, Box 1074b
MacClenny, FL 32063-9640
(904) 259-3520

Bay County Extension Office
324 West 6 Street
Panama City, FL 32401-2616
(850) 784-6105

Bradford County Extension Office
2266 N Temple Avenue
Starke, FL 32091-1028
(904) 966-6224

4-Hers sample aquatic life.

Brevard County Extension Office
3695 Lake Drive
Cocoa, FL 32926-8699
(407) 633-1702

Broward County Extension Office
3245 College Avenue
Davie, FL 33314-7798
(954) 370-3725

Calhoun County Extension Office
340 E Central Avenue
Blountstown, FL 32424-2206
(850) 674-8323

Charlotte County Extension Office
6900 Florida Street
Punta Gorda, FL 33950-5799
(941) 639-6255

Citrus County Extension Office
3600 S Florida Ave.
Inverness, FL 34450-7369
(352) 726-2141

Clay County Extension Office
2463 State Road 16 W
Green Cove Springs, FL 32043-0278
(904) 284-6355

Collier County Extension Office
14700 Immokalee Road
Naples, FL 34120-1468
(941) 353-4344

Columbia County Extension Office
PO Box 1587
Lake City, FL 32056-1587
(904) 752-5384

Dade County Extension Office
18710 SW 288 Street
Homestead, FL 33030-2309
(305) 248-3311

DeSoto County Extension Office
PO Drawer 310
Arcadia, FL 34265-0310
(941) 993-4846

Dixie County Extension Office
PO Box 640
Cross City, FL 32628-1534
(352) 498-1237

Duval County Extension Office
1010 N McDuff Ave.
Jacksonville, FL 32254-2083
(904) 387-8850

Escambia County Extension Office
3740 Stefani Road
Cantonment, FL 32533-7792
(850) 477-0953

Flagler County Extension Office
150 Sawgrass Road
Bunnell, FL 32110-9503
(904) 437-7464

Franklin County Extension Office
33 Market Street, Suite 305
Apalachicola, FL 32320-2310
(850) 653-9337

Gadsden County Extension Office
2140 W Jefferson Street
Quincy, FL 32351-1905
(850) 627-6315

Gilchrist County Extension Office
PO Box 157
Trenton, FL 32693-0157
(352) 463-3174

Glades County Extension Office
PO Box 549
Moore Haven, FL 33471-0549
(941) 946-0244

Gulf County Extension Office
200 East 2 Street
Wewahitchka, FL 32465-0250
(850) 639-3200

Hamilton County Extension Office
Drawer K
Jasper, FL 32052-0691
(904) 792-1276

Hardee County Extension Office
507 Civic Center Drive
Wauchula, FL 33873-9460
(941) 773-2164

Hendry County Extension Office
PO Box 68
Labelle, FL 33975-0068
(941) 674-4092

Hernando County Extension Office
19490 Oliver Street
Brooksville, FL 34601-6538
(352) 754-4433

Highlands County Extension Office
4509 W George Boulevard
Sebring, FL 33872-5803
(941) 386-6544

Hillsborough County Extension Office
5339 County Road 579 S
Seffner, FL 33584-3334
(813) 744-5519

Holmes County Extension Office
201 N Oklahoma Street
Bonifay, FL 32425-2295
(850) 547-1108

Indian River County Extension Office
1028 20th Place, Suite D
Vero Beach, FL 32960-5360
(561) 770-5030

Jackson County Extension Office
2741 Pennsylvania Avenue, Suite 3
Marianna, FL 32448-4014
(850) 482-9620

Jefferson County Extension Office
275 N Mulberry Street
Monticello, FL 32344-2249
(850) 342-0187

Lafayette County Extension Office
Route 3, Box 15
Mayo, FL 32066-1901
(904) 294-1279

Lake County Extension Office
30205 State Road 19
Tavares, FL 32778-4052
(352) 343-4101

Lee County Extension Office
3406 Palm Beach Boulevard
Ft. Myers, FL 33916-3719
(941) 338-3232

Leon County Extension Office
615 Paul Russell Road
Tallahassee, FL 32301-7099
(850) 487-3003

Levy County Extension Office
PO Box 219
Bronson, FL 32621-0219
(352) 486-5131

Liberty County Extension Office
PO Box 369
Bristol, FL 32321-0368
(850) 643-2229

Madison County Extension Office
900 College Avenue
Madison, FL 32340-1426
(850) 973-4138

4-H offers many programs that teach children about Florida's environment.

Manatee County Extension Office
1303 17 Street W
Palmetto, FL 34221-2998
(941) 722-4524

Marion County Extension Office
2232 NE Jacksonville Road
Ocala, FL 34470-3685
(352) 620-3440

Martin County Extension Office
2614 SE Dixie Highway
Stuart, FL 33494-4007
(561) 288-5654

Monroe County Extension Office
5100 College Road
Key West, FL 33040-4364
(305) 292-4501

Nassau County Extension Office
PO Box 1550
Callahan, FL 32011-1550
(904) 879-1019

Okaloosa County Extension Office
5479 Old Bethel Road
Crestview, FL 32536
(850) 689-5850

Okeechobee County Extension Office
458 Highway 98 N
Okeechobee, FL 34972-2303
(941) 763-6469

Orange County Extension Office
2350 E Michigan Street
Orlando, FL 32806-4996
(407) 836-7570

Osceola County Extension Office
1901 E Irlo Bronson Highway
Kissimmee, FL 34744-8947
(407) 846-4181

Palm Beach County Extension Office
559 N Military Trail
West Palm Beach, FL 33415-1131
(561) 233-1712

Pasco County Extension Office
36702 State Road 52
Dade City, FL 33525-5198
(352) 521-4288

Pinellas County Extension Office
12175 125 Street N
Largo, FL 33774-3695
(813) 582-2100

Polk County Extension Office
Drawer HS03
PO Box 9005
Bartow, FL 33831-9005
(941) 533-0765

Putnam County Extension Office
111 Yelvington Road, Suite 1
East Palatka, FL 32131-8892
(904) 329-0318

St. Johns County Extension Office
3125 Agriculture Center Drive
St. Augustine, FL 32092-0572
(904) 824-4564

St. Lucie County Extension Office
8400 Picos Road, Suite 101
Ft. Pierce, FL 34945-3045
(561) 462-1660

Santa Rosa County Extension Office
6051 Old Bagdad Highway, Room 116
Milton, FL 32583-8944
(850) 623-3868

Sarasota County Extension Office
2900 Ringling Boulevard
Sarasota, FL 34237-5397
(941) 316-1000

Mist rising from the cypress-lined lake edge of Lake Wauberg.

Florida Department of Environmental Protection

Seminole County Extension Office
250 W County Home Road
Sanford, FL 32773-6197
(407) 323-2500

Sumter County Extension Office
PO Box 218
Bushnell, FL 33513-0218
(352) 793-2728

Suwannee County Extension Office
1302 11 Street SW
Live Oak, FL 32060-3696
(904) 362-2771

Taylor County Extension Office
203 Forest Park Drive
Perry, FL 32347-6396
(850) 838-3508

Union County Extension Office
25 NE 1 Street
Lake Butler, FL 32054-1701
(904) 496-2321

Volusia County Extension Office
3100 E New York Avenue
DeLand, FL 32724-6497
(904) 822-5778

Wakulla County Extension Office
84 Cedar Avenue
Crawfordville, FL 32327-2063
(850) 926-3931

Walton County Extension Office
732 N 9 Street, Suite B
DeFuniak Springs, FL 32433-3804
(850) 892-8172

Washington County Extension Office
1424 Jackson Avenue, Suite A
Chipley, FL 32428
(850) 638-6180

*Florida LAKEWATCH
also provides citizens
with educational
material regarding their
lakes and provides a
vehicle by which
concerned citizens can
work with professionals
in government to foster
a better understanding
of Florida lakes.*

Florida LAKEWATCH

Florida LAKEWATCH is a volunteer citizen's lake monitoring program. Citizens from throughout Florida are trained by staff from the University of Florida's Department of Fisheries and Aquatic Sciences to conduct long-term scientific lake monitoring programs. Special attention is given to the monitoring of water quality and the distribution of scientifically sound lake management information. Florida LAKEWATCH also provides citizens with educational material regarding their lakes and provides a vehicle by which concerned citizens can work with professionals in government to foster a better understanding of Florida lakes.

Florida is one of many states nationwide (for example, New Hampshire, Vermont, and Wisconsin) that has a lake water quality monitoring program where long-term data are collected by citizen volunteers.

Florida is one of many states nationwide (e.g., New Hampshire, Vermont, and Wisconsin) that has a lake water quality monitoring program where long-term data are collected by citizen volunteers. Florida LAKEWATCH was started at the University of Florida in 1986. In 1990, the Florida Legislature recognized the importance of involving citizen volunteers in monitoring water quality and permanently established the Florida LAKEWATCH program within the Department of Fisheries and Aquatic Sciences of the Institute of Food and Agricultural Sciences at the University of Florida (Chapter 240.5329 F.S.). The Florida Legislature also provides sufficient in financial support annually to maintain the Florida LAKEWATCH program at approximately 600 lakes.

Florida LAKEWATCH works in cooperation with:

79 Agencies and governmental authorities

18 Businesses and professional organizations

54 Citizens groups

9 Schools

Florida LAKEWATCH reports are provided to Regional Offices of the Department of Environmental Protection, the Florida Game and Fresh Water Fish Commission and to libraries of the major Florida universities. The sixth annual report, issued in 1998, includes long-term and monthly averages for total phosphorus, total nitrogen, chlorophyll, and Secchi depth values for each lake sampled during 1997. Geologic and physiographic regions and Florida lake regions are also included. For some lakes, lake surface areas are given.

For many lakes, Florida LAKEWATCH personnel collected additional information which is provided in the 1998 report. This includes aquatic plant surveys conducted between 1991 and 1996 on approximately 300 lakes, bathymetric maps created for 40 lakes during 1996, and supplementary water chemistry data collected on over 380 lakes between 1991 and 1996 (pH, total alkalinity, conductance, color, chloride, iron, silicon, sulfate, calcium, magnesium, sodium, and potassium).

Department of Fisheries and Aquatic Sciences

The department does research, teaching, and service in the general areas of aquaculture, freshwater fisheries and limnology, and marine fisheries and ecology. Outreach activities include programs in aquaculture, fish health and disease, and freshwater fisheries and limnology. Florida LAKEWATCH is administered through the department (see address above). Call the department for more information, (352) 392-9617. Information will soon be available on the World Wide Web (http://www.ifas.ufl.edu).

> Department of Fisheries and Aquatic Sciences
> 7922 NW 71 St.
> Gainesville, FL 32653

A man-made lake can enhance your property's value.

Center for Aquatic Plants

The center deals with wetland and aquatic plants, providing information and Extension services to the public as well as to other scientists. It produces both printed and multimedia information including videotapes, newsletters, drawings and photographs of aquatic plants and aquatic plant CD-ROMs. It developed and manages the Aquatic Plant Information Retrieval System, an on-line database. Some information is free, some is for sale. Call (352) 392-1799 for more information. You also can access some of this information through the Internet (http://aquat1.ifas.ufl.edu/).

Center for Aquatic Plants
Department of Fisheries and Aquatic Sciences
7922 NW 71 St.
Gainesville, FL 32653
Tel. (352) 392-1799

Florida Aquatic Plant Society

This group of people with interest in the management of aquatic plants puts out a quarterly magazine entitled *Aquatics* which has articles related to control of aquatic plants, including effects on fishing and fish populations. For information about the magazine or the organization, contact:

Ken Langeland
Center for Aquatic Plants
7922 NW 71 St.
Gainesville, FL 32653

Florida Lake Management Society (FLMS)

FLMS is a statewide group of people interested in the welfare and management of lakes. It is a state chapter of the North American Lake Management Society, both of which are open to and encourage citizen membership as well as professionals in the area of lake management. You can become a member by joining NALMS, or you may join only the state group (FLMS).

As a member you will receive a newsletter; as a member of NALMS you will receive *LakeLine*, a citizen-oriented publication devoted to lakes and lake management (also available in university libraries). For information: Ms. Sheila Medley, FLMS, PO Box 92448, Lakeland, FL 33804-2448. The FLMS Web site is http://www.freenet.tlh.fl.us/FlLakeMgtSoc/.

North American Lake Management Society (NALMS) is an international organization dedicated to protecting and restoring lakes, ponds, and

Thomas Wright

A shoreline that is landscaped with trees attracts wildlife.

reservoirs. The Society attracts a diverse membership of citizens, lake associations, consultants, government officials, and educators. It has an increasing number of state chapters, of which FLMS (above) is one. NALMS has three major goals: 1) promote public awareness and educate citizens about what they can do to protect and preserve their lakes, ponds, and reservoirs, 2) encourage public support for national, state/provincial, and local programs promoting lake management, 3) serve as a forum for scientists to exchange informa- tion relative to lake problems and solutions. For information, write or call the NALMS Office, PO Box 5443, Madison, Wis. 53705-5443. Tel. (608) 233-2836.

Florida Department of Environmental Protection

Moss-covered trees frame a view of Paynes Prairie.

II. State of Florida

Department of Environmental Protection

This agency includes the former Department of Natural Resources and Department of Environmental Regulation. The two agencies were combined by legislative action on July 1, 1993, and the new agency has the combined responsibilities of the two former agencies. The authority of the DEP comes from a combination of state law and programs delegated by the U.S. Environmental Protection Agency. Responsibilities include natural resource conservation and protection, aquatic preserves, state parks, marine and coastal resources. Major regulatory programs relate to pollution, waste management, water resources, coastal management, and wetlands protection. The DEP's broad goals are met through three regulatory means: establishment of standards protective of natural systems, application of these standards through permitting systems which include monitoring for compliance and enforcement for non-compliance. The DEP is responsible for implementing State Water Policy (under Florida Code, Chapter 373). Specific activities relevant to water policy are carried out by the five water management districts.

The Bureau of Aquatic Plant Control is responsible for management of aquatic plants in the state's waters, including ongoing control and management plans. Regional offices and addresses are shown on the accompanying map. DEP Web site is located at http://www.dep.state.fl.us

Department of Environmental Protection
Bureau of Aquatic Plant Management
2051 East Dirac Drive, Tallahassee, FL 32310

1. Northwest Florida
   3915 Commonwealth Blvd.
   Tallahassee, FL 32399
   (904) 487-2600

2. Suwannee River
   703 North Marion Street
   Lake City, FL 32055
   (904) 758-0464

3. Southwest Florida
   6355 South Florida Ave.
   Floral City, FL 34436

4. St. Johns River
   5882 South Semoran Blvd.
   Orlando, FL 32822
   (407) 275-4004/5/6

5. South Gulf
   8302 Laurel Fair Circle
   Tampa, FL 33610
   (813) 744-6163/4

6. South Central
   2001 Homeland Garfield Rd.
   Bartow, FL 33830
   (941) 534-7074

7. South Florida
   3111 B-13 Fortune Way
   Wellington, FL 33414
   (407) 791-4720/1

Water Management Districts

There are five Water Management Districts in the state. Each is responsible for regulation and conservation of surface and ground waters within its region. Activities requiring permits from the appropriate district include water use; well construction, repair or abandonment; and dam or impoundment construction, alteration, or abandonment. Districts also have the responsibility for setting priorities for water bodies needing preservation or restoration. Districts also provide noxious aquatic weed control, following criteria set by the DEP and its Bureau of Aquatic Plant Control.

Retention ponds can provide food and refuge for many types of wildlife.

Audrey S. Wynne

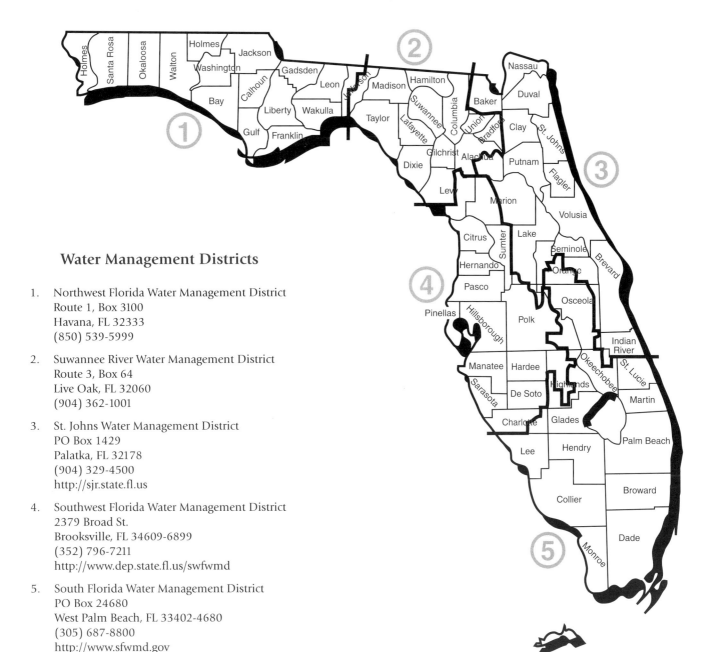

Water Management Districts

1. **Northwest Florida Water Management District**
   Route 1, Box 3100
   Havana, FL 32333
   (850) 539-5999

2. **Suwannee River Water Management District**
   Route 3, Box 64
   Live Oak, FL 32060
   (904) 362-1001

3. **St. Johns Water Management District**
   PO Box 1429
   Palatka, FL 32178
   (904) 329-4500
   http://sjr.state.fl.us

4. **Southwest Florida Water Management District**
   2379 Broad St.
   Brooksville, FL 34609-6899
   (352) 796-7211
   http://www.dep.state.fl.us/swfwmd

5. **South Florida Water Management District**
   PO Box 24680
   West Palm Beach, FL 33402-4680
   (305) 687-8800
   http://www.sfwmd.gov

Florida Game and Fresh Water Fish Commission (GFC)

This agency is concerned with managing, protecting, and conserving wild-life and freshwater aquatic life. It deals with sport and commercial fishing, fishery and habitat management, lake level drawdowns, fish stocking, and grass carp research. The GFC was established under the authority of Article 4, Section 9 of the State Constitution. Rules and regulations were defined in Chapters 39.01 and 39.192 of the Florida Administrative Code. Responsibilities include coordinating enforcement of freshwater fishing and hunting regulations, habitat restoration and monitoring, and stocking of freshwater rivers and lakes. The Web site for the GFC is located at http://sun6.dms.state.fl.us/gfc.

Marilyn D. Bachmann

Florida Game and Fresh Water Fish Commission (GFC)
620 S Meridian St., Tallahassee, FL 32399
(850) 488-1960

Division of Wildlife: (850)488-3831

Fisheries: (850)488-0331

Regional Offices

1. Northwest Regional Office
   3911 Hwy. 2321
   Panama City, FL 32409
   (850) 265-3676

2. Northeast Regional Office
   Route 7, Box 440
   Lake City, FL 32055
   (904) 752-0525

3. Central Regional Office
   1239 SW 10th St.
   Ocala, FL 34474
   (352) 732-1225

4. South Regional Office
   3900 Drane Field Rd.
   Lakeland, FL 33811
   (941) 648-3203

5. Everglades Regional Office
   8535 Northlake Blvd.
   W. Palm Beach, FL 33412
   (561) 625-5122

Florida Regional Planning Councils

Regional Planning Councils are associations of local governments. Florida is divided into four regions, each with a Planning Council. Membership includes the region's counties and its larger municipalities. One-third of the total representatives is appointed by the Governor, with the remainder appointed by member local governments. Two-thirds of the representatives must be locally elected officials.

Each Council meets monthly. Council members serve on several standing and ad hoc committees appointed by the Chairman. One of the purposes of these various committees is to advise the Council on planning and development activities which come before the Council for review and comment. The Council serves as a forum for the coordination and review of federal/state/local government, and private sector planning, development programs, and activities affecting the region.

In addition to the regional planning and review activities, the Council provides a large variety of services to benefit its local governments. These services, carried out by staff, include: technical planning assistance, grant and loan planning assistance including grant administration services, transportation planning assistance, hazardous waste monitoring, emergency response planning assistance, and economic development activities

Regional Planning Councils

1. West Florida RPC
    PO Box 486
    Pensacola, FL 32593
    Tel. (850) 595-8910
    or 1-800-226-8914
    Fax: (850) 595-8967
    http://206.105.46.100:80/wfrpc/

2. Apalachee RPC
    314 E Central Ave.
    Blountstown, FL 32424
    Tel. (850) 674-4571
    Fax (850) 674-4574
    http://www.thearpc.org/

Regional Planning Councils are associations of local governments. Florida is divided into four regions, each with a Planning Council. Membership includes the region's counties and its larger municipalities.

Regional Planning Councils (cont.)

3. North Central Florida RPC
2009 NW 67 Place, Suite A
Gainesville, FL 32653-1603
Tel. (352) 955-2200
Fax: (352) 955-2209
http://ncfrpc.org/

4. Northeast Florida RPC
8641 Baypine Rd.
Jacksonville, FL 32216
Tel. (904) 363-6350
Fax: (904) 363-6356

5. Withlacoochee RPC
1241 SW 10 St.
Ocala, FL 32674-2798
Tel. (352) 732-1315
http://www.atlantic.net/~wrpc/

6. East Central Florida RPC
1011 Wymore Rd., Suite 105
Winter Park, FL 32789
Tel. (407) 623-1075
Fax: (407) 623-1084
http://www.orlinter.com/ecfrpc/
const.htm

7. Central Florida RPC
PO Drawer 2089
Bartow, FL 33830
Tel. (941) 534-7130
or (800) 297-8041 (Florida Only)
Fax: (941) 534-7138
http://www.cfrpc.org/

8. Tampa Bay RPC
9455 Koger Blvd., Suite 209
St. Petersburg, FL 33702
(813) 577-5151

9. Southwest Florida RPC
PO Box 3455
N. Ft. Myers, FL 33918-3455
Tel. (941) 656-7720
Fax: (941) 656-7724
http://www.swfrpc.org/

10. Treasure Coast RPC
3228 SW Martin Downs Blvd., Suite 205
Palm City, FL 34990
Tel. (561) 221-4060
Fax: (561) 221-4067
http://www.tcrpc.org/rpcndx.htm

11. South Florida RPC
3440 Hollywood Blvd., Suite 140
Hollywood, FL 33021
Tel. (954) 985-4416
Fax: (954) 985-4417
http://www.sfrpc.com/

Other State Agencies of Interest

Comprehensive plans by local governments are reviewed by the Department of Community Affairs, which has jurisdiction over developmental activities affecting more than one county.

Department of Community Affairs
2740 Centerview Dr.
Tallahassee, FL 32399-2100
Tel. (904) 488-8466

This agency has responsibility for public health program administration, including public drinking water supplies and individual sewage disposal systems. Each county has an agency office which has jurisdiction within that county. The DHRS authority comes from statutes in Chapters 154, 381, and 386 of the Florida Code (the "Sanitary Code").

Department of Health and Rehabilitative Services
1317 Winewood Blvd.
Tallahassee, FL 32399-0700
Tel. (904) 488-7721

Management and protection of forests and woodlands, regulation of open burning, pesticide use, and consumer protection is provided by:

Department of Agriculture and Consumer Services
208 Mayo Building
Tallahassee, FL 32399-0800
Tel. (904) 488-2221

Florida Administrator of EPA Pesticide Regulation
Bureau of Pesticides/Division of Inspection
Department of Agriculture and Consumer Services
3125 Conner Blvd., MD-2
Tallahassee, FL 32399

*Comprehensive plans
by local governments
are reviewed by the
Department of
Community Affairs,
which has jurisdiction
over developmental
activities affecting more
than one county.*

III. Federal Agencies

U.S. Army Corps of Engineers

Part of the U.S. Army, the Corps is involved in a variety of activities. These include: responsibility for ports and inland waterways; hydroelectric power projects; providing drinking water to communities from Corps projects; the operation of recreation areas; providing permits for wetland or waterway work; work with environmental issues, monitoring and clean-up; assisting communities during natural disasters; and helping other agencies with engineering support. The Corps of Engineers Web site is located at http://www.usace.army.mil.

The Corps divides the continental United States into seven divisions. Florida is in the South Atlantic Division. Within Florida, the Corps maintains 11 regulatory offices.

Florida Regional Offices of the Corps of Engineers

1. Pensacola Regulatory Office
    160 Governmental Center
    Pensacola, FL 32501-5794
    (904) 436-8300

2. Panama City Field Office
    PO Box 151
    Panama City, FL 32402-0151
    (904) 763-0717

3. Crystal River Regulatory Office
    PO Box 387
    Crystal River, FL 32629-0387
    (904) 795-1078

4. Tampa Regulatory Office
    PO Box 19247
    Tampa, FL 33606-9247
    (813) 840-2908

5. Ft. Myers Regulatory Office
    2180 W First St.
    Can-Am Bldg., Suite 312
    Ft. Myers, FL 33901-3217
    (813) 332-7808

6. Marathon Regulatory Office
    PO Box 3238
    Marathon Shores, FL 33052-3238
    (305) 743-5349

7. Miami Regulatory Field Office
    PO Box 520766
    Miami, FL 33152-0766
    (305) 591-1302

8. Stuart Regulatory Office
    10 Central Parkway, Suite 212
    Stuart, FL 33494-2133
    (305) 286-0509

9. Merritt Island Regulatory Office
    Courtney Square Bldg., Suite 216
    2460 N. Courtney Square Blvd.
    Merritt, Island, FL 32953-4101
    (407) 453-7655

10. Palatka Regulatory Office
    PO Box 1317
    Palatka, FL 32077
    (904) 325-2028

11. Field Operations Branch
    Regulatory Division
    PO Box 4970
    Jacksonville, FL 32232
    (904) 791-3423

U.S. Environmental Protection Agency (EPA)

The EPA has programs which provide cost-sharing money for soil conservation activities and other actions to reduce pollution from non-point sources. EPA administers the Clean Lakes Program which provides cost-share money to each of the states to support work on lake restoration. See map for Florida offices (includes Florida). The EPA Web site is located at http://www.epa.gov

> Region IV Office
> 345 Courtland St. NE
> Atlanta, GA 30365

EPA National Offices & Numbers

Safe Drinking Water Hotline
(Information on regulations and programs)
1-800-426-4791

Office of Drinking Water
(Federal drinking water regulation and water wells)
401 M St. SW
Washington, DC 20460

Office of Water
(Clean Water Act and water pollution regulations)
WH 556, 401 M St. SW
Washington, DC 20460
(202) 382-5700

U.S. Fish and Wildlife Service

The work of the service includes protection of wetlands, fish and wildlife resources, endangered species. This agency, under the Department of Interior, oversees the federal fish and wildlife program authorized in the Coastal Resources Barrier Act, National Environmental Protection Act, Migratory Bird Act, Endangered Species Act, and Fish and Wildlife Coordination Act. The U.S. Fish and Wildlife Service Web site is located at http://www.fws.gov

Thomas Wright

Willows line the shore of a landscaped retention pond.

Florida is in Region 4, Southeast Region.

> U.S. Fish and Wildlife Service, Florida Office
> 16122 June Ave.
> Panama City, FL 32405-3721
> Tel. (904) 769-0552

U.S. Forest Service

This agency in the Department of Agriculture has the responsibility of managing public lands in national forests and grasslands. The Forest Service conducts research and provides both technical and financial assistance to state agencies and forestry in the private sector. The service has a Web site at http://www.fs.fed.us/

Southern Region (8) Offices	U.S. Forest Service
1720 Peachtree Rd. NW	Auditors Building
Atlanta, GA 30367	201 14 St. SW
Mailroom: R08A	Washington, DC 20250

Natural Resources Conservation Service

The U.S. Department of Agriculture's Natural Resources Conservation Service (NRCS), formerly the Soil Conservation Service, is an agency of the federal government that works with people to conserve natural resources on private lands. The agency works with rural and urban communities and individuals in partnership with conservation districts, federal and state agencies, NRCS Earth Team volunteers, Americorps members, agricultural and environmental groups, and professional societies. Their Web site can be found at http://www.ncg.nrcs.usda.gov/

> Southeast Regional Office
> 1720 Peachtree Rd. NW, Suite 446N
> Atlanta, GA 30309
> Tel. (404) 347-6105

A young family enjoys feeding the ducks at the water's edge.

Thomas Wright

This could be you...

Living at the Lake!

A Short Guide to Common Aquatic Plants in *Florida*

◄ **Alligatorweed**
(*Alternanthera philoxeroides*)
Native to South America, alligatorweed once grew completely across narrow rivers and canals. It is not as serious a pest as it once was because of insect biological control introductions. It is a sprawling emergent plant (sometimes terrestrial) that forms dense floating mats. It is characterized by opposite leaves that join and clasp the stems at their bases, hollow stems, and white papery flower cluster.

Vic Ramey

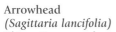

Arrowhead ►
(*Sagittaria lancifolia*)
This native emersed aquatic plant and other species of this genus are commonly used for aquascaping and mitigation planting. The showy flowers have three white petals, yellow floral parts, and occur in whorls on stalks that are up to 3 feet tall. Leaves of this species are broadly arrow-shaped but vary widely among species of the genus.

Vic Ramey

Vic Ramey

▲ **Bladderwort (*Utricularia radiata*)**
This free-floating plant can be found in ponds, lakes, swamps, and canals on the coastal plain to southern Florida. The lateral, leaf-like branches alternate and are 5 cm broad and 10 cm long. Vegetative stalks reach lengths of about 13 cm, while the stalks supporting the yellow inflorescences are only 6 cm in length. The capsular fruit sits on erect stalks and contains numerous, dark seeds. U. radiata can be distinguished from U. inflata by several factors. The inflorescence of U. radiata has 3 to 4 flowers, while the inflorescence of U. inflata has 10 to 11 flowers. Another distinguishing characteristic is the length of the floral stem. The stem that holds the inflorescence of U. radiata is 6 cm in length, while the stem of U. inflata is 15 cm long.

◀ **Cattail** (*Typha* spp.)

Three North American cattails are aggressive, pioneering species, which quickly invade disturbed areas such as newly contructed ponds, dewatered lake margins and disturbed wetlands. Strap-like leaves, which are flattened against each other at the base, grow to 8 feet tall. Tiny, brownish flowers are tightly crowned in a terminal cylindrical spike, with the male flowers above the female.

Vic Ramey

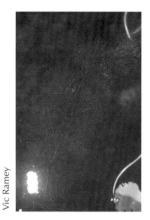

◀ **Fanwort** (*Cabomba caroliniana*)

An attractive, submersed aquatic plant, which produces two different types of leaves. Floating leaves are diamond-shaped (less than 1 inch long). Submersed leaves are opposite and divided into Y-branching segments which create a fan-shaped appearance. Flowers are white, pink, or purplish, about 1/2 inch across, and attached at the base of the floating leaves.

Vic Ramey

Eel-Grass (*Vallisneria americana*) ▶

This submerged native plant, which occurs in rivers, spring runs, and lake margins is not as common as it once was because of displacement by introduced species. It is recognized by its ribbon-like leaves, which have definite veining, some cross veins in the mid portion, and edges free of veins. Leaf tips are blunt and have a few small teeth on the leaf margins. Female flowers occur on large corkscrew-like stalks that reach the water surface. Male flowers break free and float to the surface.

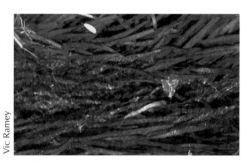

Vic Ramey

Vic Ramey and A. Murray

▲ **Fragrant Waterlily**
(*Nymphaea odorata*)

Waterlilies are probably the most popular of aquatic plants. Fragrant waterlily, a North American native, as well as other species of the genus, hybrids and cultivars, are commonly used for ornamental aquatic plantings. Fragrant waterlily is characterized by large, showy, fragrant, white (sometimes pinkish) flowers and round, floating leaves that are deeply notched and have pointed lobes.

Giant Duckweed (*Spirodela polyrhiza*) ▶

This small, free-floating plant can be found scattered throughout most of Florida. The single or multiple fronds are oblong or broadly elliptical, have five to eleven veins, are light green above, are reddish below, and have several slender roots that end in pointed root caps. One of the two reproductive pouches will produce an inflorescence that consists of one pistillated flower and two or three staminated flowers. The fruit contains one, longitudinally ribbed seed.

Vic Ramey

Vic Ramey

◀ **Giant Bulrush** (*Scirpus californicus*)

This native emersed plant is often used in lake restoration and other aquatic planting. The leafless, rounded (three-angled toward base), bright green stems can be up to 10 feet tall and arise from thick runners. The flower cluster occurs at the end of the stem but a bract appears as a continuation of the stem.

LIVING AT THE LAKE

Giant Reed
(*Phragmites australis*) ▶

This exotic grass from Africa or Australia is abundant throughout the United States. It forms dense growth along canals and often curtails bank fishing and other shoreline activities. Giant reed is used by waterfowl for cover and as a sanctuary by many birds. The stiff, erect stems are 6 to 14 feet tall with flat leaves up to 1 inch wide. Reproduction is by seed, thick rhizomes and creeping stolons.

Parrot Feather
(*Myriophyllum aquaticum*) ▶

This South American native is found primarily in central and south Florida in alkaline, hardwater, nutrient-rich lakes. The moderately long, sturdy stems of this perennial herb are both submersed and emersed. The emersed portions of this plant support grayish green whorls of leaves. The feather-like appearance of this plant is derived from the many, usually 20 or more, linear filiform divisions of the leaves. The rarely seen flowers are borne in the leaf axils. The thick, mat-like growth of this plant provides good habitat for invertebrate and fish populations.

◀ Hydrilla (*Hydrilla verticillata*)

This submersed aquatic plant is wide-spread worldwide and probably native to Africa or Asia. Since its introduction to North America, it has become the worst aquatic weed problem in the Southeastern United States. It is rapidly becoming more widespread. Hydrilla is characterized by leaves in whorls of (usually) 4 to 10 which are strap-shaped, 5/8 inch long, contain hooked teeth on the margins, and sometimes have spines or bumps on the midvein. Female flowers, which are borne near branch tips, are translucent, with 6 petals. Male flowers, which only occur in mid-Atlantic populations, break free and float on the surface.

Illinois Pondweed
(*Potamogeton illinoensis*) ▶

A native submersed plant, known to many bass anglers as peppergrass. Leaves are thin, translucent, green to brownish, up to 7 inches long and less than 2 inches wide. Flowers, which are inconspicuous, and seeds occur on compact spikes, which usually protrude above the water surface.

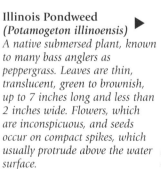

▲ Lemon Bacopa (*Bacopa caroliniana*)

This small, erect herb can be found throughout Florida. The succulent leaves are 10-30 mm long, 7-15 mm wide, opposite, ovate, and smell of lemons when they are crushed. The leaves can range from reddish-brown to lime green. The blue, solitary flowers sit on a short stem, usually 3-15 mm long, and have two green linear bracts. The fruit is a capsule that contains many seeds and is covered by the sepals. Bacopa caroliniana (lemon bacopa) can be distinguished from B. monnieri (bacopa) in two ways. Lemon bacopa has hairy stems and blue flowers, while bacopa has smooth stems and white flowers.

Pickerelweed
(Pontederia cordata)

This commonly encountered native emergent aquatic and wetland herb is often used for ornamental and mitigation plantings. Plants are usually about 3 feet tall but can reach 6 feet. The leaves tend to be in clusters and have long fleshy stalks. The blades can be narrow or broad and heart-shaped. Each stem has a leaf and a spike of numerous violet-blue (rarely white) flowers.

Vic Ramey

Water Fern
(Salvinia minima)

This small (about 3/4 inch) floating plant is a native fern. The leaves are paired, rounded, and have stiff, branched hairs on the upper surface. Thin root-like hairs hang beneath.

Vic Ramey

Spatterdock
(Nuphar luteum) ▶

This native aquatic plant, often called bonnets, is heavily fished by anglers. It is characterized by large (12 inches long), heart-shaped, emerged leaves that are attached to long stalks and large, thick underground stems. The flowers are about 1 to 1.5 inches across and bright yellow.

Vic Ramey

Water Hyacinth
(Eichhornia crassipes) ▶

Native to South America, this plant has caused severe problems when introduced into other parts of the world and has been called "the world's worst weed." It is a free-floating herb that is recognized by inflated leaf bases and clusters of purplish blue flowers on erect stalks. Plantlets may be connected by short runners. Dark, feathery, black roots hang beneath.

Vic Ramey

Torpedograss
(Panicum repens)

This non-native emersed grass is a very aggressive colonizer, which often displaces desired vegetation on lake and pond margins, and is a serious problem in drainage and irrigation canals. It can be distinguished from other aquatic grasses by its extensive underground stems that form hard, pointed, glossy-white tips. The leaves are rolled and have fine hairs on the upper surface. The seed heads are branched sharply upwards and flowers are attached individually along the branches.

Vic Ramey

Vic Ramey

Water Pennywort
(Hydrocotyle umbellata)

This commonly occurring native herb can be found throughout Florida. Its stems can grow horizontally in the mud or can float at the water's surface. The almost round blunt-toothed leaves are attached to stalks in the middle of the underside of the leaf. These leaf stalks can grow up to 300 mm in length, as can the stalks that support the small, white umbrella-shaped cluster of flowers. The fruit is a pair of nutlets that are about 3 mm long.

Glossary

Acidic - Technically, acidic liquids have an abundance of hydrogen ions. Common acidic liquids are lemon juice and vinegar. Acidic conditions can promote corrosion. See pH.

Alkaline - Alkaline liquids have a deficit of hydrogen ions. Milk is mildly alkaline. Lye, a primary consitutent of traditional drain cleaners, makes a dangerously alkaline soultion. See pH.

Alpha - A flag from the international signal alphabet, this is internationally recognized as indicating diving operations.

Aluminum - A common metal which also occurs in mineral form in lake sediments and can be dissolved in lake waters. The more acidic the water, the more aluminum it can hold.

Amphibian - A group which includes frogs, toads, and salamanders, which may live part of their lives in the water and part on land. These animals can be described as being intermediate between fishes and reptiles.

Aquascaping - Landscaping at the water's edge and into shallow waters.

Aquifer - A band of porous rock that conducts water. Much rain water that falls throughout southern Georgia and Florida finds its way into the Florida aquifer. The water in this aquifer flows from north to south.

Bathymetry - The measurement of water depth.

Berms - Raised landscaping features created as barriers to water, noise, etc.

BOD - biochemical oxygen demand. The amount of oxygen dissolved in water required by microorganisms that live in the water. The higher the BOD, the less oxygen there is for other creatures living in the water, such as fish. Organic materials, like sewage, increase BOD.

Brazilian pepper - An exotic (non-native) plant that has taken over many Florida habitats and crowded out native plant species. Scientific name: *Schinus terebinthifolius*.

Buffer - This word is used in two different ways in this book. (1) Buffers are chemicals that help resist changes in pH. (2) Buffers or buffer strips are areas of land which lie between developed and undeveloped areas to reduce the impact of development, for example, by preventing runoff from flowing directly into waterbodies.

Carbonates and bicarbonates - Chemicals composed of carbon and oxygen that are often found in minerals. Most of Florida is made of limestone which is calcium carbonate.

Channel markers - Pairs of red and green buoys that mark a navigable channel. The buoys may not always be in pairs; remember to keep the red one on your right as you come in ("red on right returning").

Chironomids - A number of kinds of small flies (midges) are chironomids. Though they are not biting flies, they can swarm in great numbers and become hazards or annoyances

Chlorophyll - The green chemical in plants that allows them to trap sunlight and convert it into chemical energy useful for growth.

Citronella - An oil that repels insects. It is often incorporated into candles. Citronella is derived from a fragrant grass that originates from Southeast Asia. Scientific name: *Cymbopogon nardus*.

CME - Courtesy Marine Exam. An examination periodically offered by the US Coast Guard. This is voluntary, but the certification can result in lower insurance rates.

Coliform bacteria - Bacteria which live in the digestive tracts of animals, present in high conentrations in sewage. These bacteria can contaminate groundwater and make it unsafe for drinking or swimming.

Corbicula - An Asiatic clam which has become naturalized in Florida displacing some native species.

Corrosion - A chemical process that gradually wears away metal parts. Rust is one kind of corrosion on iron or steel. Some metals, such as brass, are resistant to corrosion and, therefore, very useful in marine applications.

Corrosiveness - The degree to which metals are likely to corrode. See Corrosion.

DEP - Department of Environmental Protection. Florida's agency that monitors environmental quality and pollution.

Detergents - Substances which are "half water-half oil" that allow oils or greases to be dissolved and washed away from clothes, dishes, etc.

DHRS - Department of Health and Rehabilitative Services. The Florida state agency that is responsible for public health and sanitation.

Distress channel - Channel 16 VHF-FM is a reserved calling and distress channel which you can use if you need help.

Ecology - The study of how living organisms interact with their environment and with each other.

Ecosystem - A habitat with the animals and plants that live there. A community of organisms interacting with their environment. A lake is an example of an ecosystem.

Emergent macrophyte - These aquatic plants have stiff stems and grow on soils that are periodically inundated or submersed. Examples include maidencane or torpedograss (*Panicum* spp.), bulrushes (*Scirpus* spp.), cattails (*Typha* spp.), and spikerushes (*Eleocharis* spp.).

Encephalitis - An inflammation of the brain, sometimes called sleeping sickness. Two kinds of encephalitis occur in Florida, St. Louis encephalitis and Eastern equine encephalitis. Both of these viral diseases can be carried by mosquitoes and both can infect humans.

Environmental Impact Statement - Some projects require that an Environmental Impact Statement be filed with the DEP. This may be especially true if the planned development involves federal lands or a change in zoning. "Impact" is considered from several points of view in addition to possible pollution, such as noise, archaeological remains, and endangered plants or animals. Code of Federal Register (CFR) 40, Parts 1500-1508, establishes the basis for the Environmental Impact Statement.

Erlichiosis - A bacterial disease carried by the Lone Star tick. Its symptoms resemble Lyme disease, and it responds well to antibiotics.

Estuary - A body of water exposed to the sea in which salt and fresh water can mix.

Eutrophic - One of four defined trophic states of a lake characterized by high plant production.

Eutrophication - The process by which lakes can change from one trophic state to a higher one through nutrient enrichment or accumulation of nutrients.

Fatty acids - Chemicals which are "half water-half oil" (like detergents) and can help oils or greases dissolve in water where they can be rinsed away. Bar soaps are usually made of fatty acids.

Fire extinguisher - There are several kinds of fire extinguishers, but it is important to match your extinguisher to the type of fire you expect. Fires are divided into four categories, and your extinguisher will show which types of fire it is useful against. The four types of fires are:

Class A fires are those fueled by materials that leave ash when they burn. Examples: paper, wood, cloth, rubber, and certain plastics.

Class B fires involve flammable liquids and gasses, such as gasoline, paint thinner, kitchen grease, propane, or acetylene.

Class C fires involve energized electrical wiring or equipment, as in motors, computers, or panel boxes. If the electricity to the equipment is cut, a Class C fire becomes one of the other three types of fires.

Class D fires involve exotic materials: metals such as magnesium, sodium, and titanium, or specialized chemicals usually found only in laboratories.

Floating-leaved macrophyte - These plants are rooted to the lake bottom with leaves that float on the surface. Common representatives include waterlilies (*Nymphaea* spp.), spatterdock (*Nuphar* spp.), and watershield (*Brasenia* spp.).

FLMS - Florida Lake Management Society, the state chapter of the North American Lake Management Society. This group of citizens and professionals is concerned with lake welfare and management.

Floodplain - The region near a river or lake that is likely to flood under certain conditions. The expression "in the hundred-year floodplain" is often used in reference to property as a description of its tendency to be flooded.

Florida Sunshine Law - (Chapter 286, Florida Statutes) Under this law, meetings of governmental units where official actions are taken must be open to the public and minutes must be recorded.

Flushing rate - The fraction of lake volume that leaves through its outlet each year.

Fungicide - A chemical agent that kills fungus.

Free-floating macrophyte - This is a diverse group that float on or just under the water surface; they are not rooted to the bottom. Examples include tiny duckweeds (*Lemna* spp.) and water fern (*Salvinia* spp.) as well as larger plants such as water hyacinth (*Eichhornia crassipes*) and water lettuce (*Pistia stratiotes*).

General-use pesticides - Pesticides which can be applied by anyone and require no permit. Compare this to restricted-use pesticides.

Geology - The study of the earth, its history and life, in rocks. Geologists are concerned with the composition and structure of the earth.

GFC - Florida Game and Fresh Water Fish Commission. This is the state agency primarily responsible for protection and management of Florida's fish and wildlife. It is divided into units responsible for wildlife, freshwater fisheries, law enforcement, environmental services, information services and administration.

Groundwater - Water that flows through the ground, as opposed to surface waters such as rivers and streams. This water is frequently pumped through wells for drinking water.

Habitat - The environment where a plant or animal normally lives. A habitat has certain physical characteristics (such as wet or dry) that allow it to support a particular ecosystem.

Hardness - When referring to water, hardness is the total mineral content. Florida's waters generally have a moderate to high mineral content, mostly salts of calcium and magnesium.

Hazardous materials - Many manmade chemicals are in common use, and many of these pose special dangers to animals and plants if not used or disposed of carefully.

Herbicides - Chemicals that kill plants.

Humic materials - The organic component of soil. Soil is composed of inorganic materials, such as sand and clay, and organic substances that result from the decomposition of plants and animals.

Hydrilla - A non-native aquatic plant which can grow so thickly that it completely chokes water systems making them useless for navigation or recreation.

Hydrology - The study of the movements and interactions of water in the environment.

Hypereutrophic - One of four defined trophic states of a lake characterized by extremely high plant production.

Injection well - A well used to inject water into an aquifer to replace extensive withdrawals of water.

Insecticide - Chemicals used to kill insects.

Invertebrates - Animals without backbones, such as snails and worms.

Langmuir streaks - Streaks of foam that may appear on the surface of a lake. This is caused by natural action of wind and waves and does not necessarily indicate a problem.

Larvae - The early, worm-like stage that many insects go through in their development. Larvae can be aggressive, destructive feeders. (Animals other than insects may also have a larval stage.)

Leeward - The side of an object not receiving the direct force of the wind. When you are looking across a lake in the same direction as the wind is blowing (the wind is hitting the back of your head), the leeward side of the lake is the shore you are standing on. The opposite shore, which receives the force of the wind, is the windward.

Limestone - A common mineral made mostly of calcium carbonate. Most of the state of Florida is composed of limestone overlaid with clay or soil.

Liming - The use of lime to raise the pH of soil or water, in other words, to make the soil or water more alkaline and less acidic. Lime is calcium oxide which is made by heating limestone.

Limiting nutrient - In a situation where there is an abundance of most nutrients but a low supply of one nutrient is responsible for reduced growth. The one nutrient in short supply is the limiting nutrient.

Limnology - The study of lakes and rivers.

Littoral zone - The area from the lake's edge to the maximum water depth where rooted plants will grow. There are four major groups of aquatic macrophytes in the littoral zone with which you should become familiar: emergent, floating-leaved, submersed, and free-floating.

Lyme disease - A bacterial disease spread by ticks, especially *Ixodes dammini*. The first sign is often a circular rash near the bite accompanied by fever and chills. Lyme disease can be difficult to diagnose and can lead to cardiac and neurological problems.

Macrophytes - These are the plants that most people notice when they visit a lake and, potentially, the ones that cause problems. Macrophytes are a diverse group of aquatic plants encompassing flowering vascular plants, mosses, ferns, and macroalgae. They provide habitat for fish and food for waterfowl. There are four major groups of aquatic macrophytes in the littoral zone with which you should become familiar: emergent, floating-leaved, submersed, and free-floating.

Manatee protection zones - The state of Florida has established 20 zones on Florida waterways where boating access and speeds are limited. Boating accidents are the primary cause of manatee deaths.

Mercury - The only metal which is liquid at room temperature. This metal is familiar from its use in thermometers and mercury switches. Mercury is toxic and a common pollutant.

Melaleuca - A non-native tree that has invaded and dominated many regions in south Florida.

Mesotrophic - One of four defined trophic states of a lake characterized by moderate plant production.

Native birds - Protected by state and federal law, these can be taken only in accordance with regulations indicated in "Hunting Handbook Regulations Summary."

NEPA - National Environmental Policy Act. This landmark federal law was passed in 1969 and amended in 1975. Its purposes were to state a policy which encourages "harmony between man and his environment", to prevent or eliminate environmental damage and to increase "understanding of ecological systems and natural resources".

Nitrates - Nitrogen is an important nutrient for plants, and nitrates are one form of nitrogen in the environment. Nitrates are highly soluble in water and often get into groundwater in high concentrations near agricultural operations. Nitrates in your well water can be a health hazard.

Nitrogen - An important nutrient for plants.

Oligotrophic - One of four defined trophic states of a lake characterized by low plant production.

Outstanding Florida Waters - Designation for particular water bodies that gives special protection.

Parasitic - A parasite derives all or part of its nutrition from a host. Ticks are an example. This is different from symbionts which derive benefits from the host but also provide something beneficial.

Percolation - The name for the process by which water gradually works its way through the soil.

Personal watercraft ("jet skis") - Considered power boats, they must follow the same rules as larger boats. These include observing swimming areas and no-wake zones; operate only during daylight hours; have a kill switch lanyard attached to yourself; and be 14 or older (16 or older to operate a rented craft).It is also against the law to alter muffling equipment.

pH - This is a measure of the acidity or alkalinity of liquids. Technically, it is a measure of available hydrogen ions.

Photosynthesis - The process by which plants are able to capture energy from the sun and use it in chemical reactions.

Physiology - Literally, the study of the processes that go on inside living organisms. This term is often used to refer to the processes themselves.

Plankton algae - Plankton algae are small floating plants that contribute to the greenish color of nutrient-rich lakes.

Poisonous snakes - Several species of rattlesnakes, cottonmouth or water moccasin, copperhead, and coral snake.

Protected class - Wildlife and plants that are in some danger of extinction are placed in a protected class. The protected classes are: endangered, threatened, species of special concern.

Red with a white diagonal stripe (Dive flag) - Required by Florida law to indicate presence of divers. Never approach within 100 feet of any object or boat with this flag.

Regulated class - Some wildlife is protected but is of sufficient abundance so that there is limited hunting to control numbers. The alligator, which was once an endangered species, is now a regulated species. Each year, the state of Florida grants a limited number of permits to hunt alligators.

Restricted-use pesticides - You must be state-certified to get a permit to buy or apply these pesticides or to hire a commercial applicator to do so. They are restricted because, if used improperly, they could pose a danger to the operator or environment.

Revetment - A retaining wall or facing intended to prevent erosion by weather action or water.

Riparian zone - This is shoreline area included if your property lines are extended into the water .

Riparian - An adjective that refers to shore areas.

Secchi disk - A disk about eight inches diameter, usually black and white. It is used to measure water depth.

Shoreline - Average high water mark.

Sinkhole - A sinkhole is formed when underground caverns in limestone get close enough to the surface that they begin to collapse.

Solution lake - A lake formed by the action of acidic runoff.

Stormwater runoff - Applies to water flowing over buildings, streets and land's surface during and immediately after a rainstorm, carries pollutants that could degrade surface water quality.

Submersed macrophyte - These aquatic plants grow completely under water. This is a diverse group that includes quillworts (*Isoetes* spp.), mosses (*Fontinalis* spp.), muskgrasses (*Chara* spp.), stoneworts (*Nitella* spp.) and numerous vascular plants. Many submersed plants, such as widgeon-grass (*Ruppia maritima*), various pondweeds (*Potamogeton* spp.), and tape-grass (*Vallisneria* spp.) are native to the United States.

Substrate - In this book, substrate usually refers to the lake bottom.

Swale - A swale is a low area often created to guide runoff. Man-made swales are usually associated with built-up earthworks called berms.

Swamp - Swamp lands are constantly waterlogged areas that usually support tree and shrub growth.

Tannin - A common name for tannic acid. This is an organic compound common in many plants. Tannic acid is respon-

sible for the brownish color of tea. Oak leaves are especially rich in tannin, and runoff from areas with substantial oak litter is often stained brown with tannin from the leaves.

Topography - The "lay of the land." Topography is literally the shape of the land, how it rises and falls.

Toxicity - Can depend upon factors such as part of plant, season and differing reactions between individuals.

Trophic state - Trophic status related to total level of plant production (both vascular plants and algae).

Turbidity - Turbidity is the opposite of transparency. Particles suspended in water decrease transparency. Wind can re-suspend sediments, making the water turbid or muddy.

UF/IFAS Cooperative Extension - Cooperative Extension Service is a partnership of county, state and federal government which provides information and training on a full range of topics concerning people and their environment. In Florida, the Extension service is a part of the University of Florida's Institute of Food and Agricultural Sciences.

Water column of a lake - Refers to the water between the surface and the bottom.

Watershed - The area of land that drains into a stream or lake. The stream itself and its watershed are one system of many that make up a larger watershed that drains into a river.

Wetlands - A general term for land which retains water which is moving toward an open body of water. In the past, wetlands were considered nuisances and were filled indiscriminately. Now, it is apparent that wetlands perform a vital function in the environment, and more of them are being preserved.

WMD - Water Management District. The state of Florida has established a number of WMDs throughout the state to monitor and control the water resources within their districts.

Zoning - A legal process by which local governments decide how land can be used. Usually the decision is based on how surrounding property is being used.

Checklist for Buying Waterfront Property

(Adapted for Florida from the checklist in M. Dresen and R. Korth. 1994. "Living on the Edge…Owning Waterfront Property," Wisconsin Department of Natural Resources.)

There are a number of things to remember when buying waterfront property. Maybe this checklist will help you make sure all points are considered. The checklist is organized by chapter. You can quickly review the chapter if you need refreshing on any point.

Chapter 1 — Why Live at The Lake?

Why do I want to own waterfront property?

- [ ] Residence, vacation, or retirement home
- [ ] Water recreation
- [ ] Natural beauty and wildlife
- [ ] Peace and quiet
- [ ] Real estate investment

Effects on family if we move to waterfront property?

- [ ] _____

Chapter 2 — What Makes a Good Lake?

All Lakes Are Not Equal: Lake Characteristics and Differences

- [ ] Amount of macrophyte (aquatic plant) cover
- [ ] Clear or green water

Lake Ecology

- [ ] Degree of enrichment of the lake

What Kind of Lake Do You Want?

- [ ] Potential as a fishing lake
- [ ] Value as a swimming lake
- [ ] Amount of boating and water-ski activity
- [ ] Rural vs. urban setting
- [ ] Undeveloped and quiet or more activity
- [ ] Wildlife and nature observation potential

Chapter 3 — Your Wildlife Neighbors

Types of local wildlife

- [ ] Rural vs. urban wildlife problems/benefits
    - [ ] damage   [ ] safety
- [ ] Your experience/interest in wildlife
- [ ] Local problems with wildlife
- [ ] Previous owners fed birds (ducks for example) or other animals (gators or raccoons)
- [ ] Evidence of wildlife damage
- [ ] Insect/rodent damage to building or vegetation
- [ ] Exotic (non-native) plants

Noxious and Poisonous Plants

- [ ] Extensive poison ivy growth
- [ ] Other

Exotic Pests

- [ ] Presence of exotic plant problem
- [ ] Aquatic plants
- [ ] Melaleuca or Brazilian Pepper
- [ ] Exotic animal problem

Chapter 4 — Aquatic Plants

- [ ] Types and abundance of plants in water and along shore
- [ ] Do aquatic plants limit recreational use of lake?

Aquatic Plant Control

- [ ] Current plant harvesting program?
- [ ] Consult with agencies?
- [ ] Permit requirements for aquatic plant control
- [ ] Responsible agency/group and cost

Chapter 5 — Fulfilling Your Dream: Selecting and/or Developing Your Property

Time and distance to services/activities

- [ ] Emergency Services
- [ ] Shopping
- [ ] Medical care
- [ ] Repair Services
- [ ] School
- [ ] Entertainment

Other Considerations

- [ ] Land-use patterns stable or likely to change?
- [ ] Water quality suitable for my uses. Is it changing?
- [ ] Current uses of the lake (water-skiing, rowing, fishing, etc.)
- [ ] Use intensity of the lake
- [ ] Location of access facilities (boat landing, parks, camping, etc.)
- [ ] Public facilities associated with noise, litter, trespass, or other problems
- [ ] Are there variable water levels which affect use?
- [ ] Current water level: high, low or normal
- [ ] Need for flood insurance
- [ ] Higher cost for waterfront real estate

Unauthorized uses of the property

- [ ] Unrecorded rights-of-way
- [ ] Timber cutting or farming
- [ ] Camping sites
- [ ] Building encroachments
- [ ] Unsurveyed line fences
- [ ] Liens on the property?
- [ ] Unpaid real estate taxes
- [ ] Unpaid construction bills (mechanic's liens)
- [ ] Court judgements

Plans to build government facility or public utility may affect use of the property or property taxes

Possible costs

- [ ] Land and taxes
- [ ] Well
- [ ] Insurance
- [ ] Survey
- [ ] Building
- [ ] Sewage system
- [ ] Utilities/services
- [ ] Maintenance

Building Your Lakefront Home

- [ ] Reviewed applicable maps and documents
  - [ ] Soil survey
  - [ ] Topographic map
  - [ ] Plat book
  - [ ] Local zoning map and ordinance
- [ ] Viewed property during all seasons
  - [ ] Access to public road in all weather conditions
- [ ] Cost to bring utilities/access to building site
  - [ ] Electricity
  - [ ] Natural gas
  - [ ] TV (Cable /dish)
  - [ ] Fuel oil
  - [ ] Telephone
  - [ ] Access road
- [ ] Easements on the property (for private access, utilities, etc.)
- [ ] Restrictive covenants (deed restrictions)
- [ ] Property boundaries confirmed by survey

- [ ] Adequate access to the shore
- [ ] Available Contractors
  - [ ] Reputation
  - [ ] References
  - [ ] Other homes built
  - [ ] Experience with lakefront property
- [ ] Land clearing/tree removal
  - [ ] Check local ordinances
  - [ ] Environmental effects
  - [ ] Protect trees and waterfront

Your Sewage System

- [ ] New System
  - [ ] Percolation test performed and permits obtained
  - [ ] Licensed installer
  - [ ] Code compliance (setbacks, soils, size, etc.)
- [ ] Existing System
  - [ ] Location of system (plans)
  - [ ] Type of system
  - [ ] Age of system
  - [ ] Last pumping and inspection and who performed it
  - [ ] Evidence of failed system (replacement cost)
- [ ] All Sites
  - [ ] Tank construction (steel or concrete)
  - [ ] Above ground manhole locked or under-ground manhole located

- ☐ Code compliance (setbacks, size, etc.)
- ☐ Site accessible
- ☐ Soil type
- ☐ Drainfield clear of standing water
- ☐ Inspection of system
- ☐ Site available for alternate field
- ☐ Existing buffer zone
- ☐ Room to create buffer zone

A Drop to Drink...Wells

- ☐ Safe and Adequate Water (all wells)
  - ☐ Land use in surrounding area
  - ☐ Water supply safe and adequate
  - ☐ Code requirements met
  - ☐ Depth and size of well casing
  - ☐ Water flow in gallons per minute
- ☐ Problems with wells in the area
  - ☐ Low yield
  - ☐ Bacteria
  - ☐ Odor
  - ☐ Nitrate
  - ☐ Iron
  - ☐ Cloudy
  - ☐ Pesticides
  - ☐ Sulfide
  - ☐ Color
  - ☐ Radon
  - ☐ Radium

- ☐ Possible contamination sources
- ☐ Location of state certified lab for water test information and test kit
- ☐ Temporary source of drinking water until test results known

New Well

- ☐ Check out well drillers
- ☐ Permits obtained
- ☐ Well information recorded
- ☐ Pump warranty
- ☐ Copy of well log

Existing Well

- ☐ Date and results of latest water test
- ☐ Well construction records available
- ☐ Age of the well and pump
- ☐ Date pump last serviced
- ☐ Gasket-sealed well
- ☐ Distance to septic system

Docks and Boathouses

- ☐ Do docks, mooring buoys, etc. transfer
- ☐ Are structures located in owner's riparian zone
- ☐ Is property in a special district
- ☐ Suitability for boating activities
- ☐ Construction complies with federal, state and local regulations
- ☐ New construction: permit may be required

Landscaping Your Lakefront Property

- [ ] Shoreline vegetation screens buildings. Stormwater and runoff diverted/controlled
    - [ ] Berms
    - [ ] Buffer zones
    - [ ] Natural Areas
- [ ] Banks show signs of erosion
- [ ] Shoreline protection structures properly permitted and in good repair

Chapter 6 — Protecting Your Lake

- [ ] Is there a lake association?
- [ ] Existence of maintenance or restoration program
- [ ] Is the lake in a local or state monitoring program?
    - [ ] Florida LAKEWATCH
    - [ ] SWIM Program

Chapter 7 — Rights and Responsibilities of Living on the Lakefront

- [ ] Seller owns the land which borders the water
- [ ] Property includes submerged lands on a flowage, river, or stream
- [ ] Water rights transferred to third parties. History of shore trespass

Chapter 8 — Federal and State Agencies

- [ ] Development complies with federal, state, and local regulations
- [ ] Seller holds state permits for water or shoreline construction
- [ ] Conditions and terms of permits
    - [ ] Permits transferable to new owner?
    - [ ] Planned use requires state permits?
- [ ] Property enrolled in government programs that provide tax relief but restrict use?
- [ ] If located in unincorporated area, compliance with standards
    - [ ] Lot size
    - [ ] Shoreline vegetation
    - [ ] Setbacks
    - [ ] Filling and grading
- [ ] Parcel mapped as floodplain
- [ ] Floodplain zoning ordinance in place?
- [ ] Buildings located in which floodplain district?
- [ ] Structures comply with regulations?
- [ ] Flood insurance required by lender?

If there is a dam on the property

- [ ] Repair or maintenance orders
- [ ] Notices of violation
- [ ] Inspection required
- [ ] Inspection fees
- [ ] Amount of tax assessment or dues for Special Purpose Districts

Chapter 9 — The Role of Local Government

- [ ] Review zoning map and regulations
- [ ] Is intended use of the property permitted in the zoning district?
- [ ] Special zoning authorizations (variances, conditional uses, amendments) granted or denied
    - [ ] Required for planned use?
    - [ ] Unresolved zoning violations?
    - [ ] Deed restrictions
    - [ ] Zoning of nearby land?
        - [ ] Residential
        - [ ] Commercial
        - [ ] Industrial
        - [ ] Agriculture
        - [ ] Airports
        - [ ] Government projects

Chapter 10 — Water: Protection and Regulation

- [ ] Parcel mapped as wetland
- [ ] Wetland zoning ordinance in place

Chapter 11 — Recreational Laws and Regulations 1: Boating and Water Sports

- [ ] Are special boating ordinances in effect (no wake, skiing hours, etc.)?
- [ ] Is there a special waterbody designation (for example, Outstanding Florida Waterbody) which might affect use?
- [ ] Amount and effectiveness of enforcement of boating laws and regulations

Chapter 12 — Recreational Laws and Regulations 2: Fishing and Hunting

- [ ] Amount and type of recreational boating and any regulations in effect (no wake, motor sizes)
- [ ] Does the lake have any special designation which affects fishing regulations?
- [ ] Proximity of suitable hunting areas